PREPOSITIONS..

The word *preposition* implies *place before*: hence it would seem that a preposition is always *before* its object. It may be so in the majority of cases, but in a considerable proportion of instances the preposition is *after* its object.

This occurs in such cases as the following:—

> Preposition not before its object.

(1) *After a relative pronoun*, a very common occurrence; thus,—

> The most dismal Christmas fun *which* these eyes ever looked *on*.—THACKERAY.

> An ancient nation *which* they know nothing *of*.—EMERSON.

> A foe, *whom* a champion has fought *with* to-day.—SCOTT.

> Some little toys *that* girls are fond *of*.—SWIFT.

> "It's the man *that* I spoke to you *about*" said Mr. Pickwick.—DICKENS.

(2) *After an interrogative adverb, adjective, or pronoun*, also frequently found:—

> *What* God doth the wizard pray *to*?—HAWTHORNE.

> *What* is the little one thinking *about*?—J. G. HOLLAND.

> *Where* the Devil did it come *from*, I wonder?—DICKENS.

(3) *With an infinitive*, in such expressions as these:—

> A proper *quarrel* for a Crusader to do battle *in*.—SCOTT.

> "You know, General, it was *nothing* to joke *about*."—CABLE

Had no harsh *treatment* to reproach herself *with*.—BOYESEN

A *loss of vitality* scarcely to be accounted *for*.—HOLMES.

Places for *horses* to be hitched *to*.—ID.

(4) *After a noun*,—the case in which the preposition is expected to be, and regularly is, before its object; as,—

And unseen mermaids' pearly song
Comes bubbling up, the weeds *among*.
—BEDDOES.

Forever panting and forever young,
All breathing human passion far *above*.
—KEATS.

306. Since the object of a preposition is most often a noun, the statement is made that the preposition usually precedes its object; as in the following sentence, "Roused *by* the shock, he started *from* his trance."

Here the words *by* and *from* are connectives; but they do more than connect. *By* shows the relation in thought between *roused* and *shock*, expressing means or agency; *from* shows the relation in thought between *started* and *trance*, and expresses separation. Both introduce phrases.

> *Definition.*

307. A **preposition** is a word joined to a noun or its equivalent to make up a qualifying or an adverbial phrase, and to show the relation between its object and the word modified.

> *Objects, nouns and the following.*

308. Besides nouns, prepositions may have as objects—

(1) *Pronouns*: "Upon *them* with the lance;" "With *whom* I traverse earth."

(2) *Adjectives*: "On *high* the winds lift up their voices."

(3) *Adverbs*: "If I live wholly from *within*;" "Had it not been for the sea from *aft*."

(4) *Phrases*: "Everything came to her from *on high*;" "From *of old* they had been zealous worshipers."

(5) *Infinitives*: "The queen now scarce spoke to him save *to convey* some necessary command for her service."

(6) *Gerunds*: "They shrink from *inflicting* what they threaten;" "He is not content with *shining* on great occasions."

(7) *Clauses*:

> "Each soldier eye shall brightly turn
> To *where thy sky-born glories burn*."

> *Object usually objective case, if noun or pronoun.*

309. The object of a preposition, if a noun or pronoun, is usually in the objective case. In pronouns, this is shown by the form of the word, as in Sec. 308 (1).

> *Often possessive.*

In the double-possessive idiom, however, the object is in the possessive case after *of*; for example,—

> There was also a book *of Defoe's*,... and another *of Mather's*.—
> FRANKLIN.

See also numerous examples in Secs. 68 and 87.

> *Sometimes nominative.*

And the prepositions *but* and *save* are found with the nominative form of the pronoun following; as,—

> Nobody knows *but* my mate and *I*
> Where our nest and our nestlings lie.

—BRYANT.

USES OF PREPOSITIONS.

> *Inseparable.*

310. Prepositions are used in three ways:—

(1) *Compounded with verbs, adverbs,* or *conjunctions*; as, for example, with verbs, *with*draw, *under*stand, *over*look, *over*take, *over*flow, *under*go, *out*stay, *out*number, *over*run, *over*grow, etc.; with adverbs, there*at*, there*in*, there*from*, there*by*, there*with*, etc.; with conjunctions, where*at*, where*in*, where*on*, where*through*, where*upon*, etc.

> *Separable.*

(2) *Following a verb,* and being really a part of the verb. This use needs to be watched closely, to see whether the preposition belongs to the verb or has a separate prepositional function. For example, in the sentences, (*a*) "He broke a pane *from* the window," (*b*) "He broke *into* the bank," in (*a*), the verb *broke* is a predicate, modified by the phrase introduced by *from*; in (*b*), the predicate is not *broke*, modified by *into the bank*, but *broke into*—the object, *bank*.

Study carefully the following prepositions with verbs:—

Considering the space they *took up*.—SWIFT.

I loved, *laughed at*, and pitied him.—GOLDSMITH.

The sun *breaks through* the darkest clouds.—SHAKESPEARE.

They will *root up* the whole ground.—SWIFT.

A friend *prevailed upon* one of the interpreters.—ADDISON

My uncle *approved of* it.—FRANKLIN.

The robber who *broke into* them.—LANDOR.

This period is not obscurely *hinted at*.—LAMB.

The judge *winked at* the iniquity of the decision.—ID.

The pupils' voices, *conning over* their lessons.—IRVING.

To *help out* his maintenance.—ID.

With such pomp is Merry Christmas *ushered in*.—LONGFELLOW.

> *Ordinary use as connective, relation words.*

(3) As *relation words*, introducing phrases,—the most common use, in which the words have their own proper function.

> *Usefulness of prepositions.*

311. Prepositions are the subtlest and most useful words in the language for compressing a clear meaning into few words. Each preposition has its proper and general meaning, which, by frequent and exacting use, has expanded and divided into a variety of meanings more or less close to the original one.

Take, for example, the word *over*. It expresses place, with motion, as, "The bird flew *over* the house;" or rest, as, "Silence broods *over* the earth." It may also convey the meaning of *about, concerning*; as, "They quarreled *over* the booty." Or it may express time: "Stay *over* night."

The language is made richer and more flexible by there being several meanings to each of many prepositions, as well as by some of them having the same meaning as others.

CLASSES OF PREPOSITIONS.

312. It would be useless to attempt to classify all the prepositions, since they are so various in meaning.

The largest groups are those of **place**, **time**, and **exclusion**.

PREPOSITIONS OF PLACE.

313. The following are the most common to indicate **place**:—

(1) PLACE WHERE: *abaft, about, above, across, amid* (*amidst*), *among* (*amongst*), *at, athwart, below, beneath, beside, between* (*betwixt*), *beyond, in, on, over, under* (*underneath*), *upon, round* or *around, without.*

(2) PLACE WHITHER: *into, unto, up, through, throughout, to, towards.*

(3) PLACE WHENCE: *down, from* (*away from, down from, from out,* etc.), *off, out of.*

Abaft is exclusively a sea term, meaning *back of.*

Among (or **amongst**) and **between** (or **betwixt**) have a difference in meaning, and usually a difference in use. *Among* originally meant in the crowd (*on gemong*), referring to several objects; *between* and *betwixt* were originally made up of the preposition *be* (meaning *by*) and *twēon* or *twēonum* (modern *twain*), *by two,* and *be* with *twīh* (or *twuh*), having the same meaning, *by two* objects.

As to modern use, see "Syntax" (Sec. 459).

PREPOSITIONS OF TIME.

314. They are *after, during, pending, till* or *until*; also many of the prepositions of place express **time** when put before words indicating time, such as *at, between, by, about, on, within,* etc.

These are all familiar, and need no special remark.

EXCLUSION OR SEPARATION.

315. The chief ones are *besides, but, except, save, without.* The participle *excepting* is also used as a preposition.

MISCELLANEOUS PREPOSITIONS.

316. Against implies opposition, sometimes place where. In colloquial English it is sometimes used to express time, now and then also in literary

English; for example,—

> She contrived to fit up the baby's cradle for me *against* night.—Swift

About, and the participial prepositions **concerning**, **respecting**, **regarding**, mean *with reference to*.

> *Phrase prepositions.*

317. Many phrases are used as single prepositions: *by means of, by virtue of, by help of, by dint of, by force of; out of, on account of, by way of, for the sake of; in consideration of, in spite of, in defiance of, instead of, in view of, in place of; with respect to, with regard to, according to, agreeably to*; and some others.

318. Besides all these, there are some prepositions that have so many meanings that they require separate and careful treatment: *on* (*upon*), *at, by, for, from, of, to, with*.

No attempt will be made to give *all* the meanings that each one in this list has: the purpose is to stimulate observation, and to show how useful prepositions really are.

At.

319. The general meaning of **at** is *near, close to*, after a verb or expression implying position; and *towards* after a verb or expression indicating motion. It defines position approximately, while *in* is exact, meaning *within*.

Its principal uses are as follows:—

(1) *Place where.*

> They who heard it listened with a curling horror *at* the heart.—J. F. Cooper.

> There had been a strike *at* the neighboring manufacturing village, and there was to be a public meeting, *at* which he was besought to be present.—T. W. Higginson.

(2) *Time*, more exact, meaning the point of time at which.

> He wished to attack *at* daybreak.—PARKMAN.
>
> They buried him darkly, *at* dead of night.—WOLFE

(3) *Direction.*

> The mother stood looking wildly down *at* the unseemly object.
> —COOPER.
>
> You are next invited...to grasp *at* the opportunity, and take for your subject, "Health."—HIGGINSON.

Here belong such expressions as *laugh at, look at, wink at, gaze at, stare at, peep at, scowl at, sneer at, frown at,* etc.

> We *laugh at* the elixir that promises to prolong life to a thousand years.—JOHNSON.
>
> "You never mean to say," pursued Dot, sitting on the floor and *shaking* her head *at* him.—DICKENS.

(4) *Source* or *cause*, meaning *because of, by reason of.*

> I felt my heart chill *at* the dismal sound.—T. W. KNOX.
>
> Delighted *at* this outburst against the Spaniards.—PARKMAN.

(5) Then the idiomatic phrases *at last, at length, at any rate, at the best, at the worst, at least, at most, at first, at once, at all, at one, at naught, at random,* etc.; and phrases signifying state or condition of being, as, *at work, at play, at peace, at war, at rest,* etc.

Exercise.—Find sentences with three different uses of *at.*

By.

320. Like *at*, **by** means *near* or *close to,* but has several other meanings more or less connected with this,—

(1) The general meaning of *place.*

Richard was standing *by* the window.—ALDRICH.

Provided always the coach had not shed a wheel *by* the roadside.
—ID.

(2) *Time.*

But *by* this time the bell of Old Alloway began tolling.—B. TAYLOR

The angel came *by* night.—R. H. STODDARD.

(3) *Agency* or *means.*

Menippus knew which were the kings *by* their howling louder.
—M. D. CONWAY.

At St. Helena, the first port made *by* the ship, he stopped. — PARTON.

(4) *Measure of excess,* expressing the degree of difference.

At that time [the earth] was richer, *by* many a million of acres.—
DE QUINCEY.

He was taller *by* almost the breadth of my nail.—SWIFT.

(5) It is also used in *oaths and adjurations.*

By my faith, that is a very plump hand for a man of eighty-four!
—PARTON.

They implore us *by* the long trials of struggling humanity; *by* the blessed memory of the departed; *by* the wrecks of time; *by* the ruins of nations.—EVERETT.

Exercise.—Find sentences with three different meanings of *by*.

For.

321. The chief meanings of **for** are as follows:—

(1) *Motion towards* a place, or a tendency or action toward the attainment of any object.

> Pioneers who were opening the way *for* the march of the nation. —COOPER.
>
> She saw the boat headed *for* her.—WARNER.

(2) *In favor of, for the benefit of, in behalf of,* a person or thing.

> He and they were *for* immediate attack.—PARKMAN
>
> The people were then against us; they are now *for* us.—W. L. GARRISON.

(3) *Duration of time,* or *extent of space.*

> *For* a long time the disreputable element outshone the virtuous. —H. H. BANCROFT.
>
> He could overlook all the country *for* many a mile of rich woodland.—IRVING.

(4) *Substitution* or *exchange.*

> There are gains *for* all our losses.—STODDARD.
>
> Thus did the Spaniards make bloody atonement *for* the butchery of Fort Caroline.—PARKMAN.

(5) *Reference,* meaning *with regard to, as to, respecting,* etc.

> *For* the rest, the Colonna motto would fit you best.—EMERSON.
>
> *For* him, poor fellow, he repented of his folly.—E. E. HALE

This is very common with *as*—*as for* me, etc.

(6) Like *as,* meaning *in the character of, as being,* etc.

> "Nay, if your worship can accomplish that," answered Master Brackett, "I shall own you *for* a man of skill indeed!" — HAWTHORNE.

Wavering whether he should put his son to death *for* an unnatural monster.—LAMB.

(7) *Concession,* meaning *although, considering that* etc.

"*For* a fool," said the Lady of Lochleven, "thou hast counseled wisely."—SCOTT

By my faith, that is a very plump hand *for* a man of eighty-four!—PARTON.

(8) Meaning *notwithstanding,* or *in spite of.*

But the Colonel, *for* all his title, had a forest of poor relations.—HOLMES.

Still, *for* all slips of hers,
One of Eve's family.
—HOOD.

(9) *Motive, cause, reason, incitement to action.*

The twilight being...hardly more wholesome *for* its glittering mists of midge companies.—RUSKIN.

An Arab woman, but a few sunsets since, ate her child, *for* famine.—ID.

Here Satouriona forgot his dignity, and leaped *for* joy.—PARKMAN.

(10) *For* with its object preceding the infinitive, and having the same meaning as a noun clause, as shown by this sentence:—

It is by no means necessary *that he should devote his whole school existence to physical science*; nay, more, it is not necessary for *him to give up more than a moderate share of his time to such studies.*—HUXLEY.

Exercise.—Find sentences with five meanings of *for*.

From.

322. The general idea in **from** is separation or source. It may be with regard to—

(1) *Place.*

> Like boys escaped *from* school.—H. H. BANCROFT
>
> Thus they drifted *from* snow-clad ranges to burning plain.—ID.

(2) *Origin.*

> Coming *from* a race of day-dreamers, Ayrault had inherited the faculty of dreaming also by night.—HIGGINSON.
>
> *From* harmony, *from* heavenly harmony
> This universal frame began.
> —DRYDEN.

(3) *Time.*

> A distrustful, if not a desperate man, did he become *from* the night of that fearful dream—HAWTHORNE.

(4) *Motive, cause,* or *reason.*

> It was *from* no fault of Nolan's.—HALE.
>
> The young cavaliers, *from* a desire of seeming valiant, ceased to be merciful.—BANCROFT.

Exercise.—Find sentences with three meanings of *from*.

Of.

323. The original meaning of **of** was separation or source, like *from*. The various uses are shown in the following examples:—

I. The *From* Relation.

(1) *Origin or source.*

> The king holds his authority *of* the people.—MILTON.

> Thomas à Becket was born *of* reputable parents in the city of London.—HUME.

(2) *Separation*: (*a*) After certain verbs, such as *ease, demand, rob, divest, free, clear, purge, disarm, deprive, relieve, cure, rid, beg, ask*, etc.

> Two old Indians cleared the spot *of* brambles, weeds, and grass.—PARKMAN.

> Asked no odds *of,* acquitted them *of,* etc.—ALDRICH.

(*b*) After some adjectives,—*clear of, free of, wide of, bare of,* etc.; especially adjectives and adverbs of direction, as *north of, south of,* etc.

> The hills were bare *of* trees.—BAYARD TAYLOR.

> Back *of* that tree, he had raised a little Gothic chapel. — GAVARRE.

(*c*) After nouns expressing lack, deprivation, etc.

> A singular want *of* all human relation.—HIGGINSON.

(*d*) With words expressing distance.

> Until he had come within a staff's length *of* the old dame. — HAWTHORNE

> Within a few yards *of* the young man's hiding place.—ID.

(3) *With expressions of material,* especially *out of.*

White shirt with diamond studs, or breastpin *of* native gold.—BANCROFT.

Sandals, bound with thongs *of* boar's hide.—SCOTT

Who formed, *out of* the most unpromising materials, the finest army that Europe had yet seen.—MACAULAY

(4) *Expressing cause, reason, motive.*

The author died *of* a fit of apoplexy.—BOSWELL.

More than one altar was richer *of* his vows.—LEW WALLACE.

"Good for him!" cried Nolan. "I am glad *of* that."—E. E. HALE.

(5) *Expressing agency.*

You cannot make a boy know, *of* his own knowledge, that Cromwell once ruled England.—HUXLEY.

He is away *of* his own free will.—DICKENS

II. Other Relations expressed by *Of*.

(6) *Partitive*, expressing a part of a number or quantity.

Of the Forty, there were only twenty-one members present. — PARTON.

He washed out some *of* the dirt, separating thereby as much of the dust as a ten-cent piece would hold.—BANCROFT.

> *See also Sec. 309.*

(7) *Possessive*, standing, with its object, for the possessive, or being used with the possessive case to form the double possessive.

Not even woman's love, and the dignity *of* a queen, could give shelter from his contumely.—W. E. CHANNING.

And the mighty secret *of* the Sierra stood revealed.—BANCROFT.

(8) *Appositional,* which may be in the case of—

(*a*) Nouns.

> Such a book as that *of* Job.—FROUDE.
>
> The fair city *of* Mexico.—PRESCOTT.
>
> The nation *of* Lilliput.—SWIFT.

(*b*) Noun and gerund, being equivalent to an infinitive.

> In the vain hope *of* appeasing the savages.—COOPER.
>
> Few people take the trouble *of* finding out what democracy really is.—LOWELL.

(*c*) Two nouns, when the first is descriptive of the second.

> This crampfish *of* a Socrates has so bewitched him.—EMERSON
>
> A sorry antediluvian makeshift *of* a building you may think it.—LAMB.
>
> An inexhaustible bottle *of* a shop.—ALDRICH.

(9) *Of time.* Besides the phrases *of old, of late, of a sudden,* etc., *of* is used in the sense of *during.*

> I used often to linger *of* a morning by the high gate.—ALDRICH
>
> I delighted to loll over the quarter railing *of* a calm day. —IRVING.

(10) *Of reference,* equal to *about, concerning, with regard to.*

> The Turk lay dreaming *of* the hour.—HALLECK.
>
> Boasted *of* his prowess as a scalp hunter and duelist.—BANCROFT.
>
> Sank into reverie *of* home and boyhood scenes.—ID.

Idiomatic use with verbs.

Of is also used as an appendage of certain verbs, such as *admit, accept, allow, approve, disapprove, permit,* without adding to their meaning. It also accompanies the verbs *tire, complain, repent, consist, avail* (one's self), and others.

Exercise.—Find sentences with six uses of *of*.

On, Upon.

324. The general meaning of **on** is position or direction. *On* and *upon* are interchangeable in almost all of their applications, as shown by the sentences below:—

(1) *Place*: (*a*) Where.

> Cannon were heard close *on* the left.—PARKMAN.

> The Earl of Huntley ranged his host
> *Upon* their native strand.
> —MRS. SIGOURNEY.

(*b*) With motion.

> It was the battery at Samos firing *on* the boats.—PARKMAN.

> Thou didst look down *upon* the naked earth.—BRYANT.

(2) *Time.*

> The demonstration of joy or sorrow *on* reading their letters. — BANCROFT.

> *On* Monday evening he sent forward the Indians.—PARKMAN.

Upon is seldom used to express time.

(3) *Reference,* equal to *about, concerning,* etc.

> I think that one abstains from writing *on* the immortality of the soul.—EMERSON.

He pronounced a very flattering opinion *upon* my brother's promise of excellence.—DE QUINCEY.

(4) *In adjurations.*

On my life, you are eighteen, and not a day more.—ALDRICH.

Upon my reputation and credit.—SHAKESPEARE

(5) *Idiomatic phrases*: *on fire, on board, on high, on the wing, on the alert, on a sudden, on view, on trial,* etc.

Exercise.—Find sentences with three uses of *on* or *upon*.

To.

325. Some uses of to are the following:—

(1) *Expressing motion*: (*a*) To a place.

Come *to* the bridal chamber, Death!—HALLECK.

Rip had scrambled *to* one of the highest peaks.—IRVING.

(*b*) Referring to time.

Full of schemes and speculations *to* the last.—PARTON.

Revolutions, whose influence is felt *to* this hour.—PARKMAN.

(2) *Expressing result.*

He usually gave his draft to an aid...to be written over,—often *to* the loss of vigor.—BENTON

To our great delight, Ben Lomond was unshrouded.—B. TAYLOR

(3) *Expressing comparison.*

But when, unmasked, gay Comedy appears,
'Tis ten *to* one you find the girl in tears.
—ALDRICH

They are arrant rogues: Cacus was nothing *to* them.—BULWER.

Bolingbroke and the wicked Lord Littleton were saints *to* him.
—WEBSTER

(4) *Expressing concern, interest.*

To the few, it may be genuine poetry.—BRYANT.

His brother had died, had ceased to be, *to* him.—HALE.

Little mattered *to* them occasional privations—BANCROFT.

(5) *Equivalent to according to.*

Nor, *to* my taste, does the mere music...of your style fall far below the highest efforts of poetry.—LANG.

We cook the dish *to* our own appetite.—GOLDSMITH.

(6) *With the infinitive* (see Sec. 268).

Exercise.—Find sentences containing three uses of *to*.

With.

326. With expresses the idea of accompaniment, and hardly any of its applications vary from this general signification.

In Old English, *mid* meant *in company with,* while *wið* meant *against*: both meanings are included in the modern *with*.

The following meanings are expressed by *with*:—

(1) *Personal accompaniment.*

The advance, *with* Heyward at its head, had already reached the defile.—COOPER.

For many weeks I had walked *with* this poor friendless girl.—DE QUINCEY.

(2) *Instrumentality.*

With my crossbow I shot the albatross.—COLERIDGE.

Either *with* the swingle-bar, or *with* the haunch of our near leader, we had struck the off-wheel of the little gig.—DE QUINCEY.

(3) *Cause, reason, motive.*

He was wild *with* delight about Texas.—HALE.

She seemed pleased *with* the accident.—HOWELLS.

(4) *Estimation, opinion.*

How can a writer's verses be numerous if *with* him, as *with* you, "poetry is not a pursuit, but a pleasure"?—LANG.

It seemed a supreme moment *with* him.—HOWELLS.

(5) *Opposition.*

After battling *with* terrific hurricanes and typhoons on every known sea.—ALDRICH.

The quarrel of the sentimentalists is not *with* life, but *with* you.—LANG.

(6) *The equivalent of* notwithstanding, in spite of.

With all his sensibility, he gave millions to the sword.—CHANNING.

Messala, *with* all his boldness, felt it unsafe to trifle further.—WALLACE

(7) *Time.*

He expired *with* these words.—SCOTT.

With each new mind a new secret of nature transpires.—EMERSON.

Exercise.—Find sentences with four uses of *with*.

HOW TO PARSE PREPOSITIONS.

327. Since a preposition introduces a phrase and shows the relation between two things, it is necessary, first of all, to find the object of the preposition, and then to find what word the prepositional phrase limits. Take this sentence:—

> The rule adopted on board the ships on which I have met "the man without a country" was, I think, transmitted from the beginning.—E. E. HALE.

The phrases are (1) *on board the ships*, (2) *on which*, (3) *without a country*, (4) *from the beginning*. The object of *on board* is *ships*; of *on, which*; of *without, country*; of *from, beginning*.

In (1), the phrase answers the question *where*, and has the office of an adverb in telling *where* the rule is adopted; hence we say, *on board* shows the relation between *ships* and the participle *adopted*.

In (2), *on which* modifies the verb *have met* by telling where: hence *on* shows the relation between *which* (standing for *ships*) and the verb *have met*.

In (3), *without a country* modifies *man*, telling what man, or the verb *was* understood: hence *without* shows the relation between *country* and *man*, or *was*. And so on.

The **parsing** of prepositions means merely telling between what words or word groups they show relation.

Exercises.

(*a*) Parse the prepositions in these paragraphs:—

> 1. I remember, before the dwarf left the queen, he followed us one day into those gardens. I must needs show my wit by a silly illusion between him and the trees, which happens to hold in their language as it does in ours. Whereupon, the malicious rogue, watching his opportunity when I was walking under one

of them, shook it directly over my head, by which a dozen apples, each of them near as large as a Bristol barrel, came tumbling about my ears; one of them hit me on the back as I chanced to stoop, and knocked me down flat on my face; but I received no other hurt, and the dwarf was pardoned at my desire, because I had given the provocation.—SWIFT

2. Be that as it will, I found myself suddenly awakened with a violent pull upon the ring, which was fastened at the top of my box for the conveniency of carriage. I felt my box raised very high in the air, and then borne forward with prodigious speed. The first jolt had like to have shaken me out of my hammock. I called out several times, but all to no purpose. I looked towards my windows, and could see nothing but the clouds and the sky. I heard a noise just over my head, like the clapping of wings, and then began to perceive the woeful condition I was in; that some eagle had got the ring of my box in his beak, with an intent to let it fall on a rock: for the sagacity and smell of this bird enabled him to discover his quarry at a great distance, though better concealed than I could be within a two-inch board.—ID.

(b) Give the exact meaning of each italicized preposition in the following sentences:—

1. The guns were cleared *of* their lumber.

2. They then left *for* a cruise up the Indian Ocean.

3. I speak these things *from* a love of justice.

4. *To* our general surprise, we met the defaulter here.

5. There was no one except a little sunbeam *of* a sister.

6. The great gathering in the main street was *on* Sundays, when, after a restful morning, though unbroken *by* the peal of church bells, the miners gathered *from* hills and ravines *for* miles around *for* marketing.

7. The troops waited in their boats *by* the edge of a strand.

8. His breeches were *of* black silk, and his hat was garnished *with* white and sable plumes.

9. A suppressed but still distinct murmur of approbation ran through the crowd *at* this generous proposition.

10. They were shriveled and colorless *with* the cold.

11. On every solemn occasion he was the striking figure, even *to* the eclipsing of the involuntary object of the ceremony.

12. *On* all subjects known to man, he favored the world with his opinions.

13. Our horses ran *on* a sandy margin of the road.

14. The hero of the poem is *of* a strange land and a strange parentage.

15. He locked his door *from* mere force of habit.

16. The lady was remarkable *for* energy and talent.

17. Roland was acknowledged *for* the successor and heir.

18. *For* my part, I like to see the passing, in town.

19. A half-dollar was the smallest coin that could be tendered *for* any service.

20. The mother sank and fell, grasping *at* the child.

21. The savage army was in war-paint, plumed *for* battle.

22. He had lived in Paris *for* the last fifty years.

23. The hill stretched *for* an immeasurable distance.

24.

> The baron of Smaylho'me rose *with* day,
>   He spurred his courser on,
> Without stop or stay, down the rocky way
>   That leads *to* Brotherstone.

25. *With* all his learning, Carteret was far from being a pedant.

26. An immense mountain covered with a shining green turf is nothing, in this respect, *to* one dark and gloomy.

27. Wilt thou die *for* very weakness?

28. The name of Free Joe strikes humorously *upon* the ear of memory.

29. The shout I heard was *upon* the arrival of this engine.

30. He will raise the price, not merely *by* the amount of the tax.

WORDS THAT NEED WATCHING.

328. If the student has now learned fully that words must be studied in grammar according to their function or use, and not according to form, he will be able to handle some words that are used as several parts of speech. A few are discussed below,—a summary of their treatment in various places as studied heretofore.

THAT.

329. That may be used as follows:

(1) *As a demonstrative adjective.*

>*That* night was a memorable one.—STOCKTON.

(2) *As an adjective pronoun.*

>*That* was a dreadful mistake.—WEBSTER.

(3) *As a relative pronoun.*

>And now it is like an angel's song,
>*That* makes the heavens be mute.
>—COLERIDGE.

(4) *As an adverb of degree.*

>*That* far I hold that the Scriptures teach.—BEECHER.

(5) *As a conjunction*: (*a*) Of purpose.

>Has bounteously lengthened out your lives, *that* you might behold this joyous day.—WEBSTER.

(*b*) Of result.

>Gates of iron so massy *that* no man could without the help of engines open or shut them.—JOHNSON.

(*c*) Substantive conjunction.

> We wish *that* labor may look up here, and be proud in the midst of its toil.—WEBSTER.

WHAT.

330. (1) *Relative pronoun.*

> That is *what* I understand by scientific education.—HUXLEY.

(*a*) Indefinite relative.

> Those shadowy recollections,
> Which be they *what* they may,
> Are yet the fountain light of all our day.
> —WORDSWORTH.

(2) *Interrogative pronoun*: (*a*) Direct question.

> *What* would be an English merchant's character after a few such transactions?—THACKERAY.

(*b*) Indirect question.

> I have not allowed myself to look beyond the Union, to see *what* might be hidden.—WEBSTER.

(3) *Indefinite pronoun:* The saying, "I'll tell you *what*."

(4) *Relative adjective.*

> But woe to *what* thing or person stood in the way.—EMERSON.

(*a*) Indefinite relative adjective.

> To say *what* good of fashion we can, it rests on reality.—ID.

(5) *Interrogative adjective*: (*a*) Direct question.

> *What* right have you to infer that this condition was caused by the action of heat?—AGASSIZ.

(*b*) Indirect question.

> At *what* rate these materials would be distributed,...it is impossible to determine.—Iᴅ.

(6) *Exclamatory adjective.*

> Saint Mary! *what* a scene is here!—Sᴄᴏᴛᴛ.

(7) *Adverb of degree.*

> If he has [been in America], he knows *what* good people are to be found there.—Tʜᴀᴄᴋᴇʀᴀʏ.

(8) *Conjunction*, nearly equivalent to *partly... partly*, or *not only...but*.

> *What* with the Maltese goats, who go tinkling by to their pasturage; *what* with the vocal seller of bread in the early morning;...these sounds are only to be heard...in Pera.—S.S. Cox.

(9) *As an exclamation.*

> *What*, silent still, and silent all!—Bʏʀᴏɴ.

> *What*, Adam Woodcock at court!—Sᴄᴏᴛᴛ.

BUT.

331. (1) *Coördinate conjunction*: (*a*) Adversative.

> His very attack was never the inspiration of courage, *but* the result of calculation.—Eᴍᴇʀsᴏɴ.

(*b*) Copulative, after *not only*.

> Then arose not only tears, *but* piercing cries, on all sides. — Cᴀʀʟʏʟᴇ.

(2) *Subordinate conjunction*: (*a*) Result, equivalent to *that ... not*.

Nor is Nature so hard *but* she gives me this joy several times.—
EMERSON.

(*b*) Substantive, meaning *otherwise ... than*.

Who knows *but*, like the dog, it will at length be no longer traceable to its wild original—THOREAU.

(3) *Preposition*, meaning *except*.

Now there was nothing to be seen *but* fires in every direction.—LAMB.

(4) *Relative pronoun*, after a negative, stands for *that ... not*, or *who ... not*.

There is not a man in them *but* is impelled withal, at all moments, towards order.—CARLYLE.

(5) *Adverb*, meaning *only*.

The whole twenty years had been to him *but* as one night.—IRVING.

To lead *but* one measure.—SCOTT.

AS.

332. (1) *Subordinate conjunction*: (*a*) Of time.

Rip beheld a precise counterpart of himself *as* he went up the mountain.—IRVING.

(*b*) Of manner.

As orphans yearn on to their mothers,
He yearned to our patriot bands.
—MRS BROWNING.

(*c*) Of degree.

His wan eyes

Gaze on the empty scene *as* vacantly
As ocean's moon looks on the moon in heaven.
—SHELLEY.

(*d*) Of reason.

I shall see but little of it, *as* I could neither bear walking nor riding in a carriage.—FRANKLIN.

(*e*) Introducing an appositive word.

Reverenced *as* one of the patriarchs of the village.—IRVING.

Doing duty *as* a guard.—HAWTHORNE.

(2) *Relative pronoun*, after *such*, sometimes *same*.

And was there such a resemblance *as* the crowd had testified?—HAWTHORNE.

LIKE.

> *Modifier of a noun or pronoun.*

333. (1) *An adjective.*

The aforesaid general had been exceedingly *like* the majestic image.—HAWTHORNE.

They look, indeed, *liker* a lion's mane than a Christian man's locks.—SCOTT.

No Emperor, this, *like* him awhile ago.—ALDRICH.

There is no statue *like* this living man.—EMERSON.

That face, *like* summer ocean's.—HALLECK.

In each case, *like* clearly modifies a noun or pronoun, and is followed by a dative-objective.

> *Introduces a clause, but its verb is omitted.*

(2) *A subordinate conjunction* of manner. This follows a verb or a verbal, but the verb of the clause introduced by *like* is *regularly omitted*. Note the difference between these two uses. In Old English *gelic* (like) was followed by the dative, and was clearly an adjective. In this second use, *like* introduces a shortened clause modifying a verb or a verbal, as shown in the following sentences:—

> Goodman Brown came into the street of Salem village, staring *like* a bewildered man.—HAWTHORNE.

> Give Ruskin space enough, and he grows frantic and beats the air *like* Carlyle.—HIGGINSON.

> They conducted themselves much *like* the crew of a man-of-war.—PARKMAN.

> [The sound] rang in his ears *like* the iron hoofs of the steeds of Time.—LONGFELLOW.

> Stirring it vigorously, *like* a cook beating eggs.—ALDRICH.

If the verb is expressed, *like* drops out, and *as* or *as if* takes its place.

> The sturdy English moralist may talk of a Scotch supper *as* he pleases.—CASS.

> Mankind for the first seventy thousand ages ate their meat raw, just *as* they do in Abyssinia to this day.—LAMB.

> I do with my friends *as* I do with my books.—EMERSON.

NOTE.—Very rarely *like* is found with a verb following, but this is not considered good usage: for example,—

> A timid, nervous child, *like* Martin *was*.—MAYHEW.

> Through which they put their heads, *like* the Gauchos *do* through their cloaks.—DARWIN.

INTERJECTIONS.

> *Definition.*

334. Interjections are exclamations used to express emotion, and are not parts of speech in the same sense as the words we have discussed; that is, entering into the structure of a sentence.

Some of these are imitative sounds; as, tut! buzz! etc.

Humph! attempts to express a contemptuous nasal utterance that no letters of our language can really spell.

> *Not all exclamatory words are interjections.*

Other interjections are *oh*! *ah*! *alas*! *pshaw*! *hurrah*! etc. But it is to be remembered that almost any word may be used as an exclamation, but it still retains its identity as noun, pronoun, verb, etc.: for example, "Books! lighthouses built on the sea of time [noun];" "Halt! the dust-brown ranks stood fast [verb]," "Up! for shame! [adverb]," "Impossible! it cannot be [adjective]."

Analysis of Sentences

CLASSIFICATION ACCORDING TO FORM.

> *What analysis is..*

335. All discourse is made up of sentences: consequently the sentence is the unit with which we must begin. And in order to get a clear and practical idea of the structure of sentences, it is necessary to become expert in **analysis**; that is, in separating them into their component parts.

A general idea of analysis was needed in our study of the parts of speech,—in determining case, subject and predicate, clauses introduced by conjunctions, etc.

> *Value of analysis.*

A more thorough and accurate acquaintance with the subject is necessary for two reasons,—not only for a correct understanding of the principles of syntax, but for the study of punctuation and other topics treated in rhetoric.

> *Definition.*

336. A **sentence** is the expression of a thought in words.

> *Kinds of sentences as to form.*

337. According to the way in which a thought is put before a listener or reader, sentences may be of three kinds:—

(1) **Declarative**, which puts the thought in the form of a declaration or assertion. This is the most common one.

(2) **Interrogative**, which puts the thought in a question.

(3) **Imperative**, which expresses command, entreaty, or request.

Any one of these may be put in the form of an exclamation, but the sentence would still be declarative, interrogative, or imperative; hence, *according to form,* there are only the three kinds of sentences already named.

Examples of these three kinds are, declarative, "Old year, you must not die!" interrogative, "Hath he not always treasures, always friends?" imperative, "Come to the bridal chamber, Death!"

CLASSIFICATION ACCORDING TO NUMBER OF STATEMENTS

SIMPLE SENTENCES.

> *Division according to number of statements.*

338. But the division of sentences most necessary to analysis is the division, not according to the form in which a thought is put, but according to how many statements there are.

The one we shall consider first is the **simple sentence.**

> *Definition.*

339. A **simple sentence** is one which contains a single statement, question, or command: for example, "The quality of mercy is not strained;" "What wouldst thou do, old man?" "Be thou familiar, but by no means vulgar."

340. Every sentence must contain two parts,—a **subject** and a **predicate**.

> *Definition: Predicate.*

The **predicate** of a sentence is a verb or verb phrase which says something about the subject.

In order to get a correct definition of the subject, let us examine two specimen sentences:—

  1. But now all is to be changed.

  2. A rare old plant is the ivy green.

In the first sentence we find the subject by placing the word *what* before the predicate,—*What* is to be changed? Answer, *all*. Consequently, we say *all* is the subject of the sentence.

But if we try this with the second sentence, we have some trouble,—*What* is the ivy green? Answer, *a rare old plant*. But we cannot help seeing that an assertion is made, not of *a rare old plant*, but about *the ivy green*; and the real subject is the latter. Sentences are frequently in this inverted order, especially in poetry; and our definition must be the following, to suit all cases:—

> Subject.

The **subject** is that which answers the question *who* or *what* placed before the predicate, and which at the same time names that of which the predicate says something.

> The subject in interrogative and imperative simple sentences.

341. In the interrogative sentence, the subject is frequently after the verb. Either the verb is the first word of the sentence, or an interrogative pronoun, adjective, or adverb that asks about the subject. In analyzing such sentences, *always reduce them to the order of a statement*. Thus,—

(1) "When should this scientific education be commenced?"

(2) "This scientific education should be commenced when?"

(3) "What wouldst thou have a good great man obtain?"

(4) "Thou wouldst have a good great man obtain what?"

In the imperative sentence, the subject (*you, thou,* or *ye*) is in most cases omitted, and is to be supplied; as, "[You] behold her single in the field."

Exercise.

Name the subject and the predicate in each of the following sentences:—

1.
   The shadow of the dome of pleasure
   Floated midway on the waves.

2. Hence originated their contempt for terrestrial distinctions.

3. Nowhere else on the Mount of Olives is there a view like this.

4. In the sands of Africa and Arabia the camel is a sacred and precious gift.

5. The last of all the Bards was he.

6. Slavery they can have anywhere.

7. Listen, on the other hand, to an ignorant man.

8. What must have been the emotions of the Spaniards!

9. Such was not the effect produced on the sanguine spirit of the general.

10. What a contrast did these children of southern Europe present to the Anglo-Saxon races!

ELEMENTS OF THE SIMPLE SENTENCE.

342. All the **elements** of the simple sentence are as follows:—

(1) The subject.

(2) The predicate.

(3) The object.

(4) The complements.

(5) Modifiers.

(6) Independent elements.

The subject and predicate have been discussed.

343. The object may be of two kinds:—

> *Definitions. Direct Object.*

(1) The DIRECT OBJECT is that word or expression which answers the question *who* or *what* placed after the verb; or the direct object names that toward which the action of the predicate is directed.

> *Indirect object.*

(2) The INDIRECT OBJECT is a noun or its equivalent used as the modifier of a verb or verbal to name the person or thing for whose benefit an action is performed.

Examples of direct and indirect objects are, direct, "She seldom saw her *course* at a glance;" indirect, "I give *thee* this to wear at the collar."

> *Complement:*

344. A **complement** is a word added to a verb of incomplete predication to complete its meaning.

Notice that a verb of incomplete predication may be of two kinds,—transitive and intransitive.

> *Of a transitive verb.*

The *transitive verb* often requires, in addition to the object, a word to define fully the action that is exerted upon the object; for example, "Ye call me chief." Here the verb *call* has an object *me* (if we leave out *chief*), and means summoned; but *chief* belongs to the verb, and *me* here is not the object simply of *call*, but of *call chief*, just as if to say, "Ye *honor me*." This word completing a transitive verb is sometimes called a *factitive object*, or *second object*, but it is a true complement.

The fact that this is a complement can be more clearly seen when the verb is in the passive. See sentence 19, in exercise following Sec. 364.

> *Complement of an intransitive verb.*

An *intransitive verb*, especially the forms of *be, seem, appear, taste, feel, become*, etc., must often have a word to complete the meaning: as, for instance, "Brow and head were *round, and of massive weight;*" "The good man, he was now getting *old*, above sixty;" "Nothing could be *more copious* than his talk;" "But in general he seemed *deficient in laughter.*"

All these complete intransitive verbs. The following are examples of complements of transitive verbs: "Hope deferred maketh the heart *sick*;" "He was termed *Thomas*, or, more familiarly, *Thom of the Gills*;" "A plentiful fortune is reckoned *necessary*, in the popular judgment, to the completion of this man of the world."

345. The **modifiers** and **independent elements** will be discussed in detail in Secs. 351, 352, 355.

> *Phrases.*

346. A phrase is a group of words, not containing a verb, but used as a single modifier.

As to *form*, phrases are of three kinds:—

> *Three kinds.*

(1) PREPOSITIONAL, introduced by a preposition: for example, "Such a convulsion is the struggle *of gradual suffocation*, as *in drowning*; and, *in the original Opium Confessions*, I mentioned a case *of that nature*."

(2) PARTICIPIAL, consisting of a participle and the words dependent on it. The following are examples: "Then *retreating into the warm house*, and *barring the door*, she sat down to undress the two youngest children."

(3) INFINITIVE, consisting of an infinitive and the words dependent upon it; as in the sentence, "She left her home forever in order *to present herself at the Dauphin's court*."

Things used as Subject.

347. The subject of a simple sentence may be—

(1) *Noun*: "There seems to be no *interval* between greatness and meanness." Also an expression used as a noun; as, "A cheery, '*Ay, ay, sir*!' rang out in response."

(2) *Pronoun*: "We are fortified by every heroic anecdote."

(3) *Infinitive phrase*: "*To enumerate and analyze these relations* is to teach the science of method."

(4) *Gerund*: "There will be *sleeping* enough in the grave;" "What signifies *wishing* and *hoping* for better things?"

(5) *Adjective used as noun*: "*The good* are befriended even by weakness and defect;" "*The dead* are there."

(6) *Adverb*: "*Then* is the moment for the humming bird to secure the insects."

348. The subject is often found *after the verb*—

(1) *By simple inversion*: as, "Therein has been, and ever will be, my *deficiency,*—the talent of starting the game;" "Never, from their lips, was heard one *syllable* to justify," etc.

(2) *In interrogative sentences*, for which see Sec. 341.

(3) *After* "it *introductory:*" "It ought not to need *to print* in a reading room a caution not to read aloud."

In this sentence, *it* stands in the position of a grammatical subject; but the real or logical subject is *to print,* etc. It merely serves to throw the subject after a verb.

> *Disguised infinitive subject.*

There is one kind of expression that is really an infinitive, though disguised as a prepositional phrase: "It is hard *for honest men to separate* their country from their party, or their religion from their sect."

The *for* did not belong there originally, but obscures the real subject,—the infinitive phrase. Compare Chaucer: "No wonder is a lewed man to ruste" (No wonder [it] is [for] a common man to rust).

(4) *After* "there *introductory,*" which has the same office as *it* in reversing the order (see Sec. 292): "There was a *description* of the destructive operations of time;" "There are *asking eyes, asserting eyes, prowling eyes.*"

Things used as Direct Object.

349. The words used as direct object are mainly the same as those used for subject, but they will be given in detail here, for the sake of presenting examples:—

(1) *Noun*: "Each man has his own *vocation*." Also expressions used as nouns: for example, "'*By God, and by Saint George!*' said the King."

(2) *Pronoun*: "Memory greets *them* with the ghost of a smile."

(3) *Infinitive*: "We like *to see* everything do its office."

(4) *Gerund*: "She heard that *sobbing* of litanies, or the *thundering* of organs."

(5) *Adjective used as a noun*: "For seventy leagues through the mighty cathedral, I saw *the quick* and *the dead*."

Things used as Complement.

> *Complement: Of an intransitive verb.*

350. As complement of an *intransitive* verb,—

(1) *Noun*: "She had been an ardent *patriot*."

(2) *Pronoun*: "*Who* is she in bloody coronation robes from Rheims?" "This is *she*, the shepherd girl."

(3) *Adjective*: "Innocence is ever *simple* and *credulous*."

(4) *Infinitive*: "To enumerate and analyze these relations is *to teach* the science of method."

(5) *Gerund*: "Life is a *pitching* of this penny,—heads or tails;" "Serving others is *serving* us."

(6) *A prepositional phrase*: "His frame is *on a larger scale*;" "The marks were *of a kind* not to be mistaken."

It will be noticed that all these complements have a double office,—completing the predicate, and explaining or modifying the subject.

> *Of a transitive verb.*

As complement of a *transitive* verb,—

(1) *Noun*: "I will not call you *cowards*."

(2) *Adjective*: "Manners make beauty *superfluous* and *ugly*;" "Their tempers, doubtless, are rendered *pliant* and *malleable* in the fiery furnace of domestic tribulation." In this last sentence, the object is made the subject by being passive, and the words italicized are still complements. Like all the complements in this list, they are adjuncts of the object, and, at the same time, complements of the predicate.

(3) *Infinitive,* or *infinitive phrase*: "That cry which made me *look a thousand ways*;" "I hear the echoes *throng*."

(4) *Participle,* or *participial phrase*: "I can imagine him *pushing firmly on, trusting the hearts of his countrymen*."

(5) *Prepositional phrase:* "My antagonist would render my poniard and my speed *of no use* to me."

Modifiers.

I. Modifiers of Subject, Object, or Complement.

351. Since the subject and object are either nouns or some equivalent of a noun, the words modifying them must be adjectives or some equivalent of an adjective; and whenever the complement is a noun, or the equivalent of the noun, it is modified by the same words and word groups that modify the subject and the object.

These **modifiers** are as follows:—

(1) *A possessive*: "*My* memory assures me of this;" "She asked her *father's* permission."

(2) *A word in apposition*: "Theodore Wieland, the *prisoner* at the bar, was now called upon for his defense;" "Him, this young *idolater*, I have seasoned for thee."

(3) *An adjective*: "*Great* geniuses have the *shortest* biographies;" "Her father was a prince in Lebanon,—*proud, unforgiving, austere*."

(4) *Prepositional phrase*: "Are the opinions *of a man on right and wrong on fate and causation*, at the mercy of a broken sleep or an indigestion?" "The poet needs a ground *in popular tradition* to work on."

(5) *Infinitive phrase*: "The way *to know him* is to compare him, not with nature, but with other men;" "She has a new and unattempted problem *to solve*;" "The simplest utterances are worthiest *to be written*."

(6) *Participial phrase*: "Another reading, *given at the request of a Dutch lady*, was the scene from King John;" "This was the hour *already appointed for the baptism* of the new Christian daughter."

Exercise.—In each sentence in Sec. 351, tell whether the subject, object, or complement is modified.

II. Modifiers of the Predicate.

352. Since the predicate is always a verb, the word modifying it must be an adverb or its equivalent:—

(1) *Adverb:* "*Slowly* and *sadly* we laid him down."

(2) *Prepositional phrase*: "The little carriage is creeping on *at one mile an hour*;" "*In the twinkling of an eye*, our horses had carried us *to the termination of the umbrageous isle*."

In such a sentence as, "He died like a God," the word group *like a God* is often taken as a phrase; but it is really a contracted clause, the verb being omitted.

Tells how.

(3) *Participial phrase:* "She comes down from heaven to his help, *interpreting for him the most difficult truths,* and *leading him from star to star.*"

(4) *Infinitive phrase:* "No imprudent, no sociable angel, ever dropped an early syllable *to answer his longing.*"

(For participial and infinitive phrases, see further Secs. 357-363.)

(5) *Indirect object:* "I gave *every man* a trumpet;" "Give *them* not only noble teachings, but noble teachers."

These are equivalent to the phrases *to every man* and *to them,* and modify the predicate in the same way.

> *Retained with passive; or*

When the verb is changed from active to passive, the indirect object is retained, as in these sentences: "It is left *you* to find out the reason why;" "All such knowledge should be given *her.*"

> *subject of passive verb and direct object retained.*

Or sometimes the indirect object of the active voice becomes the subject of the passive, and the direct object is retained: for example, "She is to be taught *to extend the limits of her sympathy*;" "I was shown *an immense sarcophagus.*"

(6) *Adverbial objective.* These answer the question *when,* or *how long, how far,* etc., and are consequently equivalent to adverbs in modifying a predicate: "We were now running *thirteen miles an hour*;" "*One way* lies hope;" "*Four hours* before midnight we approached a mighty minster."

Exercises.

(*a*) Pick out subject, predicate, and (direct) object:—

    1. This, and other measures of precaution, I took.

2. The pursuing the inquiry under the light of an end or final cause, gives wonderful animation, a sort of personality to the whole writing.

3. Why does the horizon hold me fast, with my joy and grief, in this center?

4. His books have no melody, no emotion, no humor, no relief to the dead prosaic level.

5. On the voyage to Egypt, he liked, after dinner, to fix on three or four persons to support a proposition, and as many to oppose it.

6. Fashion does not often caress the great, but the children of the great.

7. No rent roll can dignify skulking and dissimulation.

8. They do not wish to be lovely, but to be loved.

(*b*) Pick out the subject, predicate, and complement:

1. Evil, according to old philosophers, is good in the making.

2. But anger drives a man to say anything.

3. The teachings of the High Spirit are abstemious, and, in regard to particulars, negative.

4. Spanish diet and youth leave the digestion undisordered and the slumbers light.

5. Yet they made themselves sycophantic servants of the King of Spain.

6. A merciless oppressor hast thou been.

7. To the men of this world, to the animal strength and spirits, the man of ideas appears out of his reason.

8. I felt myself, for the first time, burthened with the anxieties of a man, and a member of the world.

(*c*) Pick out the direct and the indirect object in each:—

1. Not the less I owe thee justice.

2. Unhorse me, then, this imperial rider.

3. She told the first lieutenant part of the truth.

4. I promised her protection against all ghosts.

5. I gave him an address to my friend, the attorney.

6. Paint me, then, a room seventeen feet by twelve.

(*d*) Pick out the words and phrases in apposition:—

1. To suffer and to do, that was thy portion in life.

2. A river formed the boundary,—the river Meuse.

3. In one feature, Lamb resembles Sir Walter Scott; viz., in the dramatic character of his mind and taste.

4. This view was luminously expounded by Archbishop Whately, the present Archbishop of Dublin.

5. Yes, at length the warrior lady, the blooming cornet, this nun so martial, this dragoon so lovely, must visit again the home of her childhood.

(*e*) Pick out the modifiers of the predicate:—

1. It moves from one flower to another like a gleam of light, upwards, downwards, to the right and to the left.

2.

> And hark! like the roar of the billows on the shore,
> The cry of battle rises along their changing line.

3. Their intention was to have a gay, happy dinner, after their long confinement to a ship, at the chief hotel.

4. That night, in little peaceful Easedale, six children sat by a peat fire, expecting the return of their parents.

Compound Subject, Compound Predicate, etc.

> *Not compound sentences.*

353. Frequently in a simple sentence the writer uses two or more predicates to the same subject, two or more subjects of the same predicate, several modifiers, complements, etc.; but it is to be noticed that, in all such sentences as we quote below, the writers of them purposely combined them *in single statements*, and they are not to be expanded into compound sentences. In a compound sentence the object is to make two or more full statements.

Examples of compound subjects are, "By degrees Rip's *awe* and *apprehension* subsided;" "The *name of the child, the air of the mother,* the *tone of her voice,*—all awakened a train of recollections in his mind."

Sentences with compound predicates are, "The company *broke up,* and *returned* to the more important concerns of the election;" "He *shook* his head, *shouldered* the rusty firelock, and, with a heart full of trouble and anxiety, *turned* his steps homeward."

Sentences with compound objects of the same verb are, "He caught his *daughter* and her *child* in his arms;" "*Voyages* and *travels* I would also have."

And so with complements, modifiers, etc.

Logical Subject and Logical Predicate.

354. The **logical subject** is the simple or grammatical subject, together with all its modifiers.

The **logical predicate** is the simple or grammatical predicate (that is, the verb), together with its modifiers, and its object or complement.

> *Larger view of a sentence.*

It is often a help to the student to find the logical subject and predicate first, then the grammatical subject and predicate. For example, in the sentence, "The situation here contemplated exposes a dreadful ulcer, lurking far down in the depths of human nature," the logical subject is *the situation here contemplated*, and the rest is the logical predicate. Of this, the simple subject is *situation*; the predicate, *exposes*; the object, *ulcer*, etc.

Independent Elements of the Sentence.

355. The following words and expressions are grammatically **independent** of the rest of the sentence; that is, they are not a necessary part, do not enter into its structure:—

(1) *Person or thing addressed*: "But you know them, *Bishop*;" "*Ye crags and peaks*, I'm with you once again."

(2) *Exclamatory expressions*: "But the *lady*—! Oh, *heavens*! will that spectacle ever depart from my dreams?"

> *Caution.*

The exclamatory expression, however, may be the person or thing addressed, same as (1), above: thus, "Ah, *young sir*! what are you about?" Or it may be an imperative, forming a sentence: "Oh, *hurry, hurry*, my brave young man!"

(3) *Infinitive phrase* thrown in loosely: "*To make a long story short*, the company broke up;" "*Truth to say*, he was a conscientious man."

(4) *Prepositional phrase* not modifying: "Within the railing sat, *to the best of my remembrance*, six quill-driving gentlemen;" "*At all events*, the great man of the prophecy had not yet appeared."

(5) *Participial phrase:* "But, *generally speaking*, he closed his literary toils at dinner;" "*Considering the burnish of her French tastes*, her noticing even this is creditable."

(6) *Single words*: as, "Oh, *yes*! everybody knew them;" "*No*, let him perish;" "*Well*, he somehow lived along;" "*Why*, grandma, how you're winking!" "*Now*, this story runs thus."

> *Another caution.*

There are some adverbs, such as *perhaps, truly, really, undoubtedly, besides*, etc., and some conjunctions, such as *however, then, moreover, therefore, nevertheless*, etc., that have an office in the sentence, and should not be confused with the words spoken of above. The words *well, now, why*, and so on, are independent when they merely arrest the attention without being necessary.

PREPOSITIONAL PHRASES.

356. In their use, prepositional phrases may be,

(1) *Adjectival*, modifying a noun, pronoun, or word used as a noun: for example, "He took the road *to King Richard's pavilion*;" "I bring reports *on that subject* from Ascalon."

(2) *Adverbial*, limiting in the same way an adverb limits: as, "All nature around him slept *in calm moonshine* or *in deep shadow*;" "Far *from the madding crowd's ignoble strife*."

(3) *Independent*, not dependent on any word in the sentence (for examples, see Sec. 355, 4).

PARTICIPLES AND PARTICIPIAL PHRASES.

357. It will be helpful to sum up here the results of our study of participles and participial phrases, and to set down all the uses which are of importance in analysis:—

(1) *The adjectival use*, already noticed, as follows:—

> (*a*) As a complement of a transitive verb, and at the same time a modifier of the object (for an example, see Sec. 350, 4).

> (*b*) As a modifier of subject, object, or complement (see Sec. 351, 6).

(2) *The adverbial use*, modifying the predicate, instances of which were seen in Sec. 352, 3. In these the participial phrases connect closely with the verb, and there is no difficulty in seeing that they modify.

> *These need close watching.*

There are other participial phrases which are used adverbially, but require somewhat closer attention; thus, "The letter of introduction, *containing no matters of business*, was speedily run through."

In this sentence, the expression *containing no matters of business* does not describe *letter*, but it is equivalent to *because it contained no matters of business*, and hence is adverbial, modifying *was speedily run through*.

Notice these additional examples:—

Being a great collector of everything relating to Milton [reason, "Because I was," etc.], I had naturally possessed myself of Richardson the painter's thick octavo volumes.

Neither the one nor the other writer was valued by the public, *both having* [since they had] *a long warfare to accomplish of contumely and ridicule*.

Wilt thou, therefore, *being now wiser* [as thou art] *in thy thoughts*, suffer God to give by seeming to refuse?

(3) *Wholly independent* in meaning and grammar. See Sec. 355, (5), and these additional examples:—

Assuming the specific heat to be the same as that of water, the entire mass of the sun would cool down to 15,000° Fahrenheit in five thousand years.

This case excepted, the French have the keenest possible sense of everything odious and ludicrous in posing.

INFINITIVES AND INFINITIVE PHRASES.

358. The various uses of the infinitive give considerable trouble, and they will be presented here in full, or as nearly so as the student will require.

I. The verbal use. (1) Completing an incomplete verb, but having no other office than a verbal one.

(*a*) With *may (might),can (could),should,would,seem, ought,* etc.: "My weekly bill used invariably *to be* about fifty shillings;" "There, my dear, he should not *have known* them at all;" "He would *instruct* her in the white man's religion, and *teach* her how to be happy and good."

(*b*) With the forms of *be*, being equivalent to a future with obligation, necessity, etc.: as in the sentences, "Ingenuity and cleverness are *to be rewarded* by State prizes;" "'The Fair Penitent' was *to be acted* that evening."

(*c*) With the definite forms of *go*, equivalent to a future: "I was going *to repeat* my remonstrances;" "I am not going *to dissert* on Hood's humor."

(2) Completing an incomplete transitive verb, but also belonging to a subject or an object (see Sec. 344 for explanation of the complements of transitive verbs): "I am constrained every moment *to acknowledge* a higher origin for events" (retained with passive); "Do they not cause the heart *to beat*, and the eyes *to fill*?"

359. II. The substantive use, already examined; but see the following examples for further illustration:—

(1) *As the subject:* "*To have* the wall there, was to have the foe's life at their mercy;" "*To teach* is to learn."

(2) *As the object*: "I like *to hear* them tell their old stories;" "I don't wish *to detract* from any gentleman's reputation."

(3) *As complement:* See examples under (1), above.

(4) *In apposition*, explanatory of a noun preceding: as, "She forwarded to the English leaders a touching invitation *to unite* with the French;" "He insisted on his right *to forget* her."

360. III. The adjectival use, modifying a noun that may be a subject, object, complement, etc.: for example, "But there was no time *to be lost*;"

"And now Amyas had time *to ask* Ayacanora the meaning of this;" "I have such a desire *to be* well with my public" (see also Sec. 351, 5).

361. IV. The adverbial use, which may be to express—

(1) *Purpose:* "The governor, Don Guzman, sailed to the eastward only yesterday *to look* for you;" "Isn't it enough to bring us to death, *to please* that poor young gentleman's fancy?"

(2) *Result:* "Don Guzman returns to the river mouth *to find* the ship a blackened wreck;" "What heart could be so hard as *not to take* pity on the poor wild thing?"

(3) *Reason:* "I am quite sorry *to part* with them;" "Are you mad, *to betray* yourself by your own cries?" "Marry, hang the idiot, *to bring me* such stuff!"

(4) *Degree:* "We have won gold enough *to serve* us the rest of our lives;" "But the poor lady was too sad *to talk* except to the boys now and again."

(5) *Condition:* "You would fancy, *to hear* McOrator after dinner, the Scotch fighting all the battles;" "*To say* what good of fashion we can, it rests on reality" (the last is not a simple sentence, but it furnishes a good example of this use of the infinitive).

362. The fact that the infinitives in Sec. 361 are used adverbially, is evident from the meaning of the sentences.

Whether each sentence containing an adverbial infinitive has the meaning of purpose, result, etc., may be found out by turning the infinitive into an equivalent clause, such as those studied under subordinate conjunctions.

To test this, notice the following:—

In (1), *to look* means *that he might look*; *to please* is equivalent to *that he may please*,—both purpose clauses.

In (2), *to find* shows the result of the return; *not to take pity* is equivalent to *that it would not take pity*.

In (3), *to part* means *because I part*, etc.; and *to betray* and *to bring* express the reason, equivalent to *that you betray*, etc.

In (4), *to serve* and *to talk* are equivalent to [*as much gold*] *as will serve us*; and "too sad *to talk*" also shows degree.

In (5), *to hear* means *if you should hear*, and *to say* is equivalent to *if we say*,—both expressing condition.

363. V. The independent use, which is of two kinds,—

(1) Thrown loosely into the sentence; as in Sec. 355, (3).

(2) *Exclamatory:* "I a philosopher! I *advance* pretensions;" "'He *to die!*' resumed the bishop." (See also Sec. 268, 4.)

OUTLINE OF ANALYSIS.

364. In analyzing simple sentences, give—

(1) The predicate. If it is an incomplete verb, give the complement (Secs. 344 and 350) and its modifiers (Sec. 351).

(2) The object of the verb (Sec. 349).

(3) Modifiers of the object (Sec. 351).

(4) Modifiers of the predicate (Sec. 352).

(5) The subject (Sec. 347).

(6) Modifiers of the subject (Sec. 351).

(7) Independent elements (Sec. 355).

This is not the same order that the parts of the sentence usually have; but it is believed that the student will proceed more easily by finding the predicate with its modifiers, object, etc., and then finding the subject by placing the question *who* or *what* before it.

Exercise in Analyzing Simple Sentences.

Analyze the following according to the directions given:—

1. Our life is March weather, savage and serene in one hour.

2. I will try to keep the balance true.

3. The questions of Whence? What? and Whither? and the solution of these, must be in a life, not in a book.

4. The ward meetings on election days are not softened by any misgiving of the value of these ballotings.

5. Our English Bible is a wonderful specimen of the strength and music of the English language.

6. Through the years and the centuries, through evil agents, through toys and atoms, a great and beneficent tendency irresistibly streams.

7. To be hurried away by every event, is to have no political system at all.

8. This mysticism the ancients called ecstasy,—a getting-out of their bodies to think.

9. He risked everything, and spared nothing, neither ammunition, nor money, nor troops, nor generals, nor himself.

10. We are always in peril, always in a bad plight, just on the edge of destruction, and only to be saved by invention and courage.

11. His opinion is always original, and to the purpose.

12. To these gifts of nature, Napoleon added the advantage of having been born to a private and humble fortune.

13.

>   The water, like a witch's oils,
>   Burnt green and blue and white.

14. We one day descried some shapeless object floating at a distance.

15.

> Old Adam, the carrion crow,
>   The old crow of Cairo;
> He sat in the shower, and let it flow
>   Under his tail and over his crest.

16. It costs no more for a wise soul to convey his quality to other men.

17. It is easy to sugar to be sweet.

18. At times the black volume of clouds overhead seemed rent asunder by flashes of lightning.

19. The whole figure and air, good and amiable otherwise, might be called flabby and irresolute.

20. I have heard Coleridge talk, with eager energy, two stricken hours, and communicate no meaning whatsoever to any individual.

21. The word *conscience* has become almost confined, in popular use, to the moral sphere.

22. You may ramble a whole day together, and every moment discover something new.

23. She had grown up amidst the liberal culture of Henry's court a bold horsewoman, a good shot, a graceful dancer, a skilled musician, an accomplished scholar.

24. Her aims were simple and obvious,—to preserve her throne, to keep England out of war, to restore civil and religious order.

25.

> Fair name might he have handed down,
> Effacing many a stain of former crime.

26. Of the same grandeur, in less heroic and poetic form, was the patriotism of Peel in recent history.

27. Oxford, ancient mother! hoary with ancestral honors, time-honored, and, haply, time-shattered power—I owe thee nothing!

28. The villain, I hate him and myself, to be a reproach to such goodness.

29. I dare this, upon my own ground, and in my own garden, to bid you leave the place now and forever.

30. Upon this shore stood, ready to receive her, in front of all this mighty crowd, the prime minister of Spain, the same Condé Olivarez.

31. Great was their surprise to see a young officer in uniform stretched within the bushes upon the ground.

32. She had made a two days' march, baggage far in the rear, and no provisions but wild berries.

33. This amiable relative, an elderly man, had but one foible, or perhaps one virtue, in this world.

34. Now, it would not have been filial or ladylike.

35. Supposing this computation to be correct, it must have been in the latitude of Boston, the present capital of New England.

36. The cry, "A strange vessel close aboard the frigate!" having already flown down the hatches, the ship was in an uproar.

37.

> But yield, proud foe, thy fleet
> With the crews at England's feet.

38. Few in number, and that number rapidly perishing away through sickness and hardships; surrounded by a howling wilderness and savage tribes; exposed to the rigors of an almost arctic winter,—their minds were filled with doleful forebodings.

39. List to the mournful tradition still sung by the pines of the forest.

40.

> In the Acadian land, on the shores of the Basin of Minas,
> Distant, secluded, still, the little village of Grand-Pré
> Lay in the fruitful valley.

41. Must we in all things look for the how, and the why, and the wherefore?

CONTRACTED SENTENCES.

> *Words left out after* than *or* as.

365. Some sentences look like simple ones in form, but have an essential part omitted that is so readily supplied by the mind as not to need expressing. Such are the following:—

"There is no country more worthy of our study than England [is worthy of our study]."

"The distinctions between them do not seem to be so marked as [they are marked] in the cities."

To show that these words are really omitted, compare with them the two following:—

"The nobility and gentry are more popular among the inferior orders than *they are* in any other country."

"This is not so universally the case at present as *it was* formerly."

> *Sentences with* like.

366. As shown in Part I. (Sec. 333). the expressions *of manner* introduced by *like*, though often treated as phrases, are really contracted clauses; but, if they were expanded, *as* would be the connective instead of *like*; thus,—

"They'll shine o'er her sleep, like [as] a smile from the west
    [would shine].
From her own loved island of sorrow."

This must, however, be carefully discriminated from cases where *like* is an adjective complement; as,—

"She is *like* some tender tree, the pride and beauty of the grove;"
"The ruby seemed *like* a spark of fire burning upon her white bosom."

Such contracted sentences form a connecting link between our study of simple and complex sentences.

COMPLEX SENTENCES.

> *The simple sentence the basis.*

367. Our investigations have now included all the machinery of the simple sentence, which is the *unit of speech*.

Our further study will be in sentences which are combinations of simple sentences, made merely for convenience and smoothness, to avoid the tiresome repetition of short ones of monotonous similarity.

Next to the simple sentence stands the complex sentence. The basis of it is two or more simple sentences, which are so united that one member is the main one,—the backbone,—the other members subordinate to it, or dependent on it; as in this sentence,—

"When such a spirit breaks forth into complaint, we are aware how great must be the suffering that extorts the murmur."

The relation of the parts is as follows:—

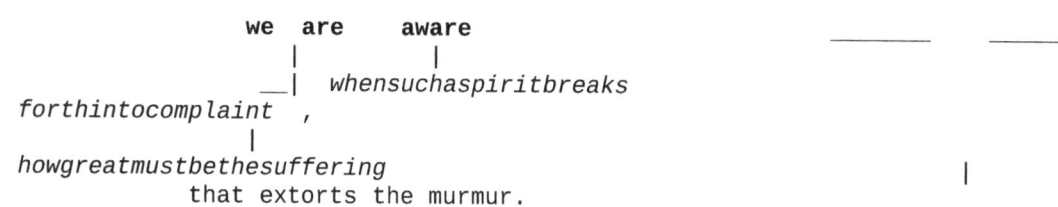

This arrangement shows to the eye the picture that the sentence forms in the mind,—how the first clause is held in suspense by the mind till the second, **we are aware**, is taken in; then we recognize this as the main statement; and the next one, *how great ... suffering*, drops into its place as subordinate to *we are aware*; and the last, *that ... murmur*, logically depends on *suffering*.

Hence the following definition:—

> *Definition.*

368. A **complex sentence** is one containing one main or independent clause (also called the principal proposition or clause), and *one or more* subordinate or dependent clauses.

369. The **elements** of a complex sentence are the same as those of the simple sentence; that is, each clause has its subject, predicate, object, complements, modifiers, etc.

But there is this difference: whereas the simple sentence always has a word or a phrase for subject, object, complement, and modifier, the complex sentence has *statements* or *clauses* for these places.

CLAUSES.

> *Definition.*

370. A clause is a division of a sentence, containing a verb with its subject.

Hence the term *clause* may refer to the main division of the complex sentence, or it may be applied to the others,—the dependent or subordinate clauses.

> *Independent clause.*

371. A **principal, main**, or **independent clause** is one making a statement without the help of any other clause.

> *Dependent clause.*

A **subordinate** or **dependent clause** is one which makes a statement depending upon or modifying some word in the principal clause.

> *Kinds.*

372. As to their office in the sentence, clauses are divided into NOUN, ADJECTIVE, and ADVERB clauses, according as they are equivalent in use to nouns, adjectives, or adverbs.

Noun Clauses.

373. Noun clauses have the following uses:—

(1) *Subject*: "*That such men should give prejudiced views of America* is not a matter of surprise."

(2) *Object of a verb, verbal, or the equivalent of a verb*: (*a*) "I confess *these stories, for a time, put an end to my fancies*;" (*b*) "I am aware [I know] *that a skillful illustrator of the immortal bard would have swelled the materials*."

Just as the object noun, pronoun, infinitive, etc., is retained after a passive verb (Sec. 352, 5), so the object clause is retained, and should not be called an adjunct of the subject; for example, "We are persuaded *that a thread runs through all things*;" "I was told *that the house had not been shut, night or day, for a hundred years*."

(3) *Complement*: "The terms of admission to this spectacle are, *that he have a certain solid and intelligible way of living*."

(4) *Apposition*. (*a*) Ordinary apposition, explanatory of some noun or its equivalent: "Cecil's saying of Sir Walter Raleigh, '*I know that he can toil terribly*,' is an electric touch."

(*b*) After "it *introductory*" (logically this is a subject clause, but it is often treated as in apposition with *it*): "*It* was the opinion of some, *that this might be the wild huntsman famous in German legend*."

(5) *Object of a preposition*: "At length he reached to *where the ravine had opened through the cliffs*."

Notice that frequently only the introductory word is the object of the preposition, and the whole clause is not; thus, "The rocks presented a high impenetrable wall, *over which* the torrent came tumbling."

> "Alas! it is we ourselves that are getting buried alive under this avalanche of earthly impertinences."

To divide this into two clauses—(*a*) *It is we ourselves*, (*b*) *that are ... impertinences*—would be grammatical; but logically the sentence is, *We ourselves are getting ... impertinences*, and *it is ... that* is merely a framework used to effect emphasis. The sentence shows how *it* may lose its pronominal force.

Other examples of this construction are,—

> "It is on the understanding, and not on the sentiment, of a nation, that all safe legislation must be based."

> "Then it is that deliberative Eloquence lays aside the plain attire of her daily occupation."

Exercise.

Tell how each noun clause is used in these sentences:—

1. I felt that I breathed an atmosphere of sorrow.

2. But the fact is, I was napping.

3. Shaking off from my spirit what must have been a dream, I scanned more narrowly the aspect of the building.

4. Except by what he could see for himself, he could know nothing.

5. Whatever he looks upon discloses a second sense.

6. It will not be pretended that a success in either of these kinds is quite coincident with what is best and inmost in his mind.

7. The reply of Socrates, to him who asked whether he should choose a wife, still remains reasonable, that, whether he should choose one or not, he would repent it.

8. What history it had, how it changed from shape to shape, no man will ever know.

9. Such a man is what we call an original man.

10. Our current hypothesis about Mohammed, that he was a scheming impostor, a falsehood incarnate, that his religion is a mere mass of quackery and fatuity, begins really to be no longer tenable to any one.

Adjective Clauses.

375. As the office of an adjective is to modify, the only use of an adjective clause is to limit or describe some noun, or equivalent of a noun: consequently the adjective may modify *any* noun, or equivalent of a noun, in the sentence.

The adjective clause may be introduced by the relative pronouns *who, which, that, but, as*; sometimes by the conjunctions *when, where, whither, whence, wherein, whereby*, etc.

Frequently there is no connecting word, a relative pronoun being understood.

> *Examples of adjective clauses.*

376. Adjective clauses may modify—

(1) *The subject*: "The themes *it offers for contemplation* are too vast for their capacities;" "Those *who see the Englishman only in town*, are apt to form an unfavorable opinion of his social character."

(2) *The object*: "From this piazza Ichabod entered the hall, *which formed the center of the mansion*."

(3) *The complement*: "The animal he bestrode was a broken-down plow-horse, *that had outlived almost everything but his usefulness*;" "It was such an apparition *as is seldom to be met with in broad daylight*."

(4) *Other words*: "He rode with short stirrups, *which brought his knees nearly up to the pommel of the saddle*;" "No whit anticipating the oblivion

which awaited their names and feats, the champions advanced through the lists;" "Charity covereth a multitude of sins, in another sense than that *in which it is said to do so in Scripture.*"

Exercise.

Pick out the adjective clauses, and tell what each one modifies; i.e., whether subject, object, etc.

1. There were passages that reminded me perhaps too much of Massillon.

2. I walked home with Calhoun, who said that the principles which I had avowed were just and noble.

3. Other men are lenses through which we read our own minds.

4. In one of those celestial days when heaven and earth meet and adorn each other, it seems a pity that we can only spend it once.

5. One of the maidens presented a silver cup, containing a rich mixture of wine and spice, which Rowena tasted.

6. No man is reason or illumination, or that essence we were looking for.

7. In the moment when he ceases to help us as a cause, he begins to help us more as an effect.

8. Socrates took away all ignominy from the place, which could not be a prison whilst he was there.

9. This is perhaps the reason why we so seldom hear ghosts except in our long-established Dutch settlements.

10. From the moment you lose sight of the land you have left, all is vacancy.

11. Nature waited tranquilly for the hour to be struck when man should arrive.

Adverbial Clauses.

377. The adverb clause takes the place of an adverb in modifying a verb, a verbal, an adjective, or an adverb. The student has met with many adverb clauses in his study of the subjunctive mood and of subordinate conjunctions; but they require careful study, and will be given in detail, with examples.

378. Adverb clauses are of the following kinds:

(1) TIME: "*As we go,* the milestones are grave-stones;" "He had gone but a little way *before he espied a foul fiend coming;*" "*When he was come up to Christian,* he beheld him with a disdainful countenance."

(2) PLACE: "*Wherever the sentiment of right comes in,* it takes precedence of everything else;" "He went several times to England, *where he does not seem to have attracted any attention.*"

(3) REASON, or CAUSE: "His English editor lays no stress on his discoveries, *since he was too great to care to be original;*" "I give you joy *that truth is altogether wholesome.*"

(4) MANNER: "The knowledge of the past is valuable only *as it leads us to form just calculations with respect to the future;*" "After leaving the whole party under the table, he goes away *as if nothing had happened.*"

(5) DEGREE, or COMPARISON: "They all become wiser *than they were;*" "The right conclusion is, that we should try, so far *as we can,* to make up our shortcomings;" "Master Simon was in as chirping a humor *as a grasshopper filled with dew* [is];" "*The broader their education is,* the wider is the horizon of their thought." The first clause in the last sentence is dependent, expressing the degree in which the horizon, etc., is wider.

(6) PURPOSE: "Nature took us in hand, shaping our actions, *so that we might not be ended untimely by too gross disobedience.*"

(7) RESULT, or CONSEQUENCE: "He wrote on the scale of the mind itself, *so that all things have symmetry in his tablet;*" "The window was so far superior to every other in the church, *that the vanquished artist killed himself from mortification.*"

(8) CONDITION: "*If we tire of the saints*, Shakespeare is our city of refuge;" "Who cares for that, *so thou gain aught wider and nobler*?" "You can die grandly, and as goddesses would die *were goddesses mortal*."

(9) CONCESSION, introduced by indefinite relatives, adverbs, and adverbial conjunctions,—*whoever, whatever, however,* etc.: "But still, *however good she may be as a witness*, Joanna is better;" "*Whatever there may remain of illiberal in discussion,* there is always something illiberal in the severer aspects of study."

These mean *no matter how good, no matter what remains*, etc.

Exercise.

Pick out the adverbial clauses in the following sentences; tell what kind each is, and what it modifies:—

1. As I was clearing away the weeds from this epitaph, the little sexton drew me on one side with a mysterious air, and informed me in a low voice that once upon a time, on a dark wintry night, when the wind was unruly, howling and whistling, banging about doors and windows, and twirling weathercocks, so that the living were frightened out of their beds, and even the dead could not sleep quietly in their graves, the ghost of honest Preston was attracted by the well-known call of "waiter," and made its sudden appearance just as the parish clerk was singing a stave from the "mirrie garland of Captain Death."

2. If the children gathered about her, as they sometimes did, Pearl would grow positively terrible in her puny wrath, snatching up stones to fling at them, with shrill, incoherent exclamations, that made her mother tremble because they had so much the sound of a witch's anathemas.

3. The spell of life went forth from her ever-creative spirit, and communicated itself to a thousand objects, as a torch kindles a flame wherever it may be applied.

ANALYZING COMPLEX SENTENCES.

379. These suggestions will be found helpful:—

(1) See that the sentence and all its parts are placed in the natural order of subject, predicate, object, and modifiers.

(2) First take the sentence *as a whole*; find the principal subject and principal predicate; then treat noun clauses as nouns, adjective clauses as adjectives modifying certain words, and adverb clauses as single modifying adverbs.

(3) Analyze each clause as a simple sentence. For example, in the sentence, "Cannot we conceive that Odin was a reality?" *we* is the principal subject; *cannot conceive* is the principal predicate; its object is *that Odin was a reality*, of which clause *Odin* is the subject, etc.

380. It is sometimes of great advantage to map out a sentence after analyzing it, so as to picture the parts and their relations. To take a sentence:—

> "I cannot help thinking that the fault is in themselves, and that if the church and the cataract were in the habit of giving away their thoughts with that rash generosity which characterizes tourists, they might perhaps say of their visitors, 'Well, if you are those men of whom we have heard so much, we are a little disappointed, to tell the truth.'"

This may be represented as follows:—

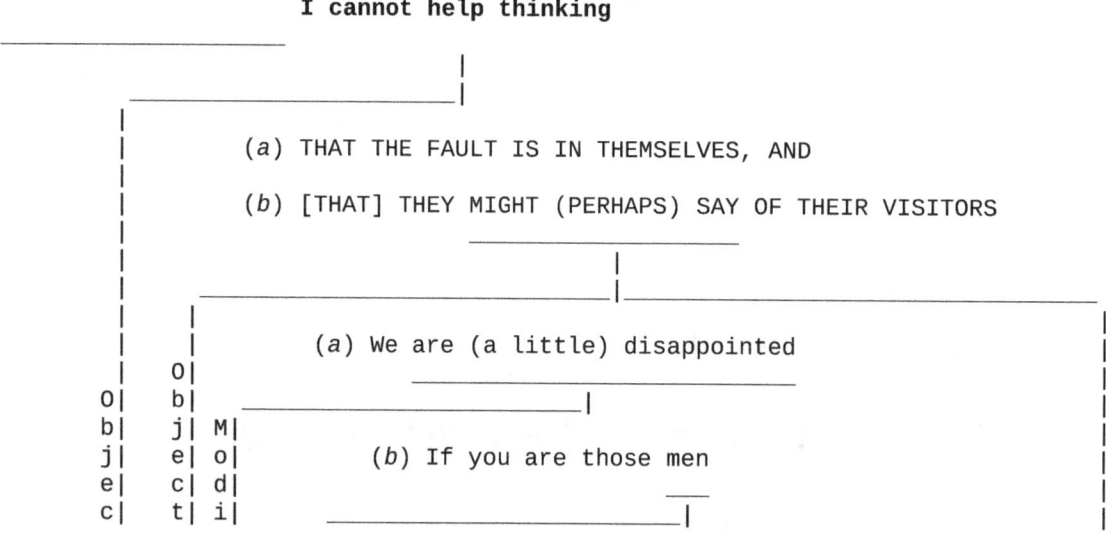

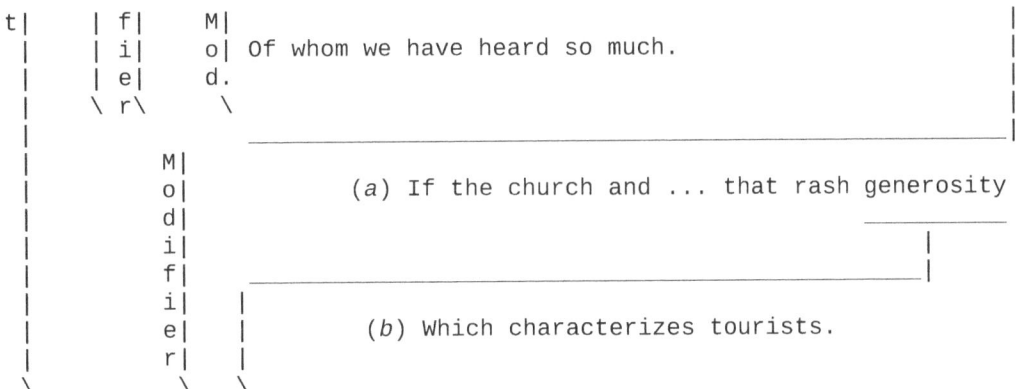

OUTLINE

381. (1) Find the principal clause.

(2) Analyze it according to Sec. 364.

(3) Analyze the dependent clauses according to Sec. 364. This of course includes dependent clauses that depend on other dependent clauses, as seen in the "map" (Sec. 380).

Exercises.

(*a*) Analyze the following complex sentences:—

    1. Take the place and attitude which belong to you.

    2. That mood into which a friend brings us is his dominion over us.

    3. True art is only possible on the condition that every talent has its apotheosis somewhere.

    4. The deep eyes, of a light hazel, were as full of sorrow as of inspiration.

    5. She is the only church that has been loyal to the heart and soul of man, that has clung to her faith in the imagination.

    6. She has never lost sight of the truth that the product human nature is composed of the sum of flesh and spirit.

7. But now that she has become an establishment, she begins to perceive that she made a blunder in trusting herself to the intellect alone.

8. Before long his talk would wander into all the universe, where it was uncertain what game you would catch, or whether any.

9. The night proved unusually dark, so that the two principals had to tie white handkerchiefs round their elbows in order to descry each other.

10. Whether she would ever awake seemed to depend upon an accident.

11. Here lay two great roads, not so much for travelers that were few, as for armies that were too many by half.

12. It was haunted to that degree by fairies, that the parish priest was obliged to read mass there once a year.

13. More than one military plan was entered upon which she did not approve.

14. As surely as the wolf retires before cities, does the fairy sequester herself from the haunts of the licensed victualer.

15. M. Michelet is anxious to keep us in mind that this bishop was but an agent of the English.

16. Next came a wretched Dominican, that pressed her with an objection, which, if applied to the Bible, would tax every miracle with unsoundness.

17. The reader ought to be reminded that Joanna D'Arc was subject to an unusually unfair trial.

18. Now, had she really testified this willingness on the scaffold, it would have argued nothing at all but the weakness of a genial nature.

19. And those will often pity that weakness most, who would yield to it least.

20. Whether she said the word is uncertain.

21. This is she, the shepherd girl, counselor that had none for herself, whom I choose, bishop, for yours.

22. Had *they* been better chemists, had *we* been worse, the mixed result, namely, that, dying for *them*, the flower should revive for *us*, could not have been effected.

23. I like that representation they have of the tree.

24. He was what our country people call *an old one*.

25. He thought not any evil happened to men of such magnitude as false opinion.

26. These things we are forced to say, if we must consider the effort of Plato to dispose of Nature,—which will not be disposed of.

27. He showed one who was afraid to go on foot to Olympia, that it was no more than his daily walk, if continuously extended, would easily reach.

28. What can we see or acquire but what we are?

29. Our eyes are holden that we cannot see things that stare us in the face, until the hour arrives when the mind is ripened.

30. There is good reason why we should prize this liberation.

(b) First analyze, then map out as in Sec. 380, the following complex sentences:—

1. The way to speak and write what shall not go out of fashion, is to speak and write sincerely.

2. The writer who takes his subject from his ear, and not from his heart, should know that he has lost as much as he has gained.

3. "No book," said Bentley, "was ever written down by any but itself."

4. That which we do not believe, we cannot adequately say, though we may repeat the words never so often.

5. We say so because we feel that what we love is not in your will, but above it.

6. It makes no difference how many friends I have, and what content I can find in conversing with each, if there be one to whom I am not equal.

7. In every troop of boys that whoop and run in each yard and square, a new-comer is as well and accurately weighed in the course of a few days, and stamped with his right number, as if he had undergone a formal trial of his strength, speed, and temper.

COMPOUND SENTENCES.

> *How formed.*

382. The **compound sentence** is a combination of two or more simple or complex sentences. While the complex sentence has only *one* main clause, the compound has *two or more* independent clauses making statements, questions, or commands. Hence the definition,—

> *Definition.*

383. A **compound sentence** is one which contains two or more independent clauses.

This leaves room for any number of subordinate clauses in a compound sentence: the requirement is simply that it have at least two independent clauses.

Examples of compound sentences:—

> *Examples.*

(1) *Simple sentences united:* "He is a palace of sweet sounds and sights; he dilates; he is twice a man; he walks with arms akimbo; he soliloquizes."

(2) *Simple with complex:* "The trees of the forest, the waving grass, and the peeping flowers have grown intelligent; and he almost fears to trust them with the secret which they seem to invite."

(3) *Complex with complex:* "The power which resides in him is new in nature, and none but he knows what that is which he can do, nor does he know until he has tried."

384. From this it is evident that nothing new is added to the work of analysis already done.

The same analysis of simple sentences is repeated in (1) and (2) above, and what was done in complex sentences is repeated in (2) and (3).

The division into members will be easier, for the coördinate independent statements are readily taken apart with the subordinate clauses attached, if there are any.

Thus in (1), the semicolons cut apart the independent members, which are simple statements; in (2), the semicolon separates the first, a simple member, from the second, a complex member; in (3), *and* connects the first and second complex members, and *nor* the second and third complex members.

Connectives.

385. The coördinate conjunctions *and, nor, or but*, etc., introduce independent clauses (see Sec. 297).

But the conjunction is often omitted in copulative and adversative clauses, as in Sec. 383 (1). Another example is, "Only the star dazzles; the planet has a faint, moon-like ray" (adversative).

Study the thought.

386. The one point that will give trouble is the variable use of some connectives; as *but, for, yet, while (whilst), however, whereas*, etc. Some of these are now conjunctions, now adverbs or prepositions; others sometimes coördinate, sometimes subordinate conjunctions.

The student must watch *the logical connection* of the members of the sentence, and not the form of the connective.

Exercise.

Of the following illustrative sentences, tell which are compound, and which complex:—

1. Speak your latent conviction, and it shall be the universal sense; for the inmost in due time becomes the outmost.

2. I no longer wish to meet a good I do not earn, for example, to find a pot of buried gold.

3. Your goodness must have some edge to it—else it is none.

4. Man does not stand in awe of man, nor is his genius admonished to stay at home, but it goes abroad to beg a cup of water of the urns of other men.

5. A man cannot speak but he judges himself.

6. In your metaphysics you have denied personality to the Deity, yet when the devout motions of the soul come, yield to them heart and life.

7. I thought that it was a Sunday morning in May; that it was Easter Sunday, and as yet very early in the morning.

8. We denote the primary wisdom as intuition, whilst all later teachings are tuitions.

9. Whilst the world is thus dual, so is every one of its parts.

10. They measure the esteem of each other by what each has, and not by what each is.

11. For everything you have missed, you have gained something else; and for everything you gain, you lose something.

12. I sometimes seemed to have lived for seventy or one hundred years in one night; nay, I sometimes had feelings representative of a millennium, passed in that time, or, however, of a duration far beyond the limits of experience.

13. However some may think him wanting in zeal, the most fanatical can find no taint of apostasy in any measure of his.

14. In this manner, from a happy yet often pensive child, he grew up to be a mild, quiet, unobtrusive boy, and sun-browned with labor in the fields, but with more intelligence than is seen in many lads from the schools.

OUTLINE FOR ANALYZING COMPOUND SENTENCES.

387. (i) Separate it into its main members. (2) Analyze each complex member as in Sec. 381. (3) Analyze each simple member as in Sec. 364.

Exercise.

Analyze the following compound sentences:—

1. The gain is apparent; the tax is certain.

2. If I feel overshadowed and outdone by great neighbors, I can yet love; I can still receive; and he that loveth maketh his own the grandeur that he loves.

3. Love, and thou shalt be loved.

4. All loss, all pain, is particular; the universe remains to the heart unhurt.

5. Place yourself in the middle of the stream of power and wisdom which animates all whom it floats, and you are without effort impelled to truth.

6. He teaches who gives, and he learns who receives.

7. Whatever he knows and thinks, whatever in his apprehension is worth doing, that let him communicate, or men will never know and honor him aright.

8. Stand aside; give those merits room; let them mount and expand.

9. We see the noble afar off, and they repel us; why should we intrude?

10. We go to Europe, or we pursue persons, or we read books, in the instinctive faith that these will call it out and reveal us to ourselves.

11. A gay and pleasant sound is the whetting of the scythe in the mornings of June, yet what is more lonesome and sad than the sound

of a whetstone or mower's rifle when it is too late in the season to make hay?

12. "Strike," says the smith, "the iron is white;" "keep the rake," says the haymaker, "as nigh the scythe as you can, and the cart as nigh the rake."

13. Trust men, and they will be true to you; treat them greatly, and they will show themselves great, though they make an exception in your favor to all their rules of trade.

14. On the most profitable lie the course of events presently lays a destructive tax; whilst frankness invites frankness, puts the parties on a convenient footing, and makes their business a friendship.

15. The sturdiest offender of your peace and of the neighborhood, if you rip up his claims, is as thin and timid as any; and the peace of society is often kept, because, as children, one is afraid, and the other dares not.

16. They will shuffle and crow, crook and hide, feign to confess here, only that they may brag and conquer there, and not a thought has enriched either party, and not an emotion of bravery, modesty, or hope.

17. The magic they used was the ideal tendencies, which always make the Actual ridiculous; but the tough world had its revenge the moment they put their horses of the sun to plow in its furrow.

18. Come into port greatly, or sail with God the seas.

19. When you have chosen your part, abide by it, and do not weakly try to reconcile yourself with the world.

20. Times of heroism are generally times of terror, but the day never shines in which this element may not work.

21. Life is a train of moods like a string of beads, and as we pass through them they prove to be many-colored lenses which paint the world their own hue, and each shows only what lies at its focus.

22. We see young men who owe us a new world, so readily and lavishly they promise, but they never acquit the debt; they die young, and dodge the account; or, if they live, they lose themselves in the crowd.

23. So does culture with us; it ends in headache.

24. Do not craze yourself with thinking, but go about your business anywhere.

25. Thus journeys the mighty Ideal before us; it never was known to fall into the rear.

Syntax

INTRODUCTORY.

By way of introduction.

388. Syntax is from a Greek word meaning *order* or *arrangement.*

Syntax deals with the relation of words to each other as component parts of a sentence, and with their proper arrangement to express clearly the intended meaning.

Ground covered by syntax.

380. Following the Latin method, writers on English grammar usually divide syntax into the two general heads,—**agreement** and **government**.

Agreement is concerned with the following relations of words: words in apposition, verb and subject, pronoun and antecedent, adjective and noun.

Government has to do with verbs and prepositions, both of which are said to govern words by having them in the objective case.

390. Considering the scarcity of inflections in English, it is clear that if we merely follow the Latin treatment, the department of syntax will be a small affair. But there is a good deal else to watch in addition to the few forms; for there is an important and marked difference between Latin and English syntax. It is this:—

Latin syntax depends upon fixed rules governing the use of inflected forms: hence the *position* of words in a sentence is of little grammatical importance.

Essential point in English syntax.

English syntax follows the Latin to a limited extent; but its leading characteristic is, that English syntax is founded upon *the meaning* and *the logical connection* of words rather than upon their form: consequently it is quite as necessary to place words properly, and to think clearly of the meaning of words, as to study inflected forms.

For example, the sentence, "The savage here the settler slew," is ambiguous. *Savage* may be the subject, following the regular order of subject; or *settler* may be the subject, the order being inverted. In Latin, distinct forms would be used, and it would not matter which one stood first.

> *Why study syntax?*

391. There is, then, a double reason for not omitting syntax as a department of grammar,—

First, To study the rules regarding the use of inflected forms, some of which conform to classical grammar, while some are idiomatic (peculiar to our own language).

Second, To find out the *logical methods* which control us in the arrangement of words; and particularly when the grammatical and the logical conception of a sentence do not agree, or when they exist side by side in good usage.

As an illustration of the last remark, take the sentence, "Besides these famous books of Scott's and Johnson's, there is a copious 'Life' by Sheridan." In this there is a possessive form, and added to it the preposition *of,* also expressing a possessive relation. This is not logical; it is not consistent with the general rules of grammar: but none the less it is good English.

Also in the sentence, "None remained but he," grammatical rules would require *him* instead of *he* after the preposition; yet the expression is sustained by good authority.

> *Some rules not rigid.*

392. In some cases, authorities—that is, standard writers—differ as to which of two constructions should be used, or the same writer will use both indifferently. Instances will be found in treating of the pronoun or noun with a gerund, pronoun and antecedent, sometimes verb and subject, etc.

When usage varies as to a given construction, both forms will be given in the following pages.

> *The basis of syntax.*

393. Our treatment of syntax will be an endeavor to record the best usage of the present time on important points; and nothing but important points will be considered, for it is easy to confuse a student with too many obtrusive *don'ts*.

The constructions presented as general will be justified by quotations from *modern writers of English* who are regarded as "standard;" that is, writers whose style is generally acknowledged as superior, and whose judgment, therefore, will be accepted by those in quest of authoritative opinion.

Reference will also be made to spoken English when its constructions differ from those of the literary language, and to vulgar English when it preserves forms which were once, but are not now, good English.

It may be suggested to the student that the only way to acquire correctness is to watch good usage *everywhere*, and imitate it.

NOUNS.

394. Nouns have no distinct forms for the nominative and objective cases: hence no mistake can be made in using them. But some remarks are required concerning the use of the possessive case.

> *Use of the possessive. Joint possession.*

395. When two or more possessives modify the same noun, or indicate joint ownership or possession, the possessive sign is added to the last noun only; for example,—

> Live your *king and country's* best support.—ROWE.

> Woman, *sense and nature's* easy fool.—BYRON.

> *Oliver and Boyd's* printing office.—MCCULLOCH.

> *Adam and Eve's* morning hymn.—MILTON.

> In *Beaumont and Fletcher's* "Sea Voyage," Juletta tells, etc.— EMERSON.

> *Separate possession.*

396. When two or more possessives stand before the same noun, but imply separate possession or ownership, the possessive sign is used with each noun; as,—

> He lands us on a grassy stage, Safe from the *storm's* and *prelate's* rage.—MARVELL

> Where were the sons of Peers and Members of Parliament in *Anne's* and *George's* time?—THACKERAY.

> *Levi's* station in life was the receipt of custom; and *Peter's*, the shore of Galilee; and *Paul's*, the antechamber of the High Priest. —RUSKIN.

Swift did not keep *Stella's* letters. He kept *Bolingbroke's*, and *Pope's*, and *Harley's*, and *Peterborough's*.—THACKERAY.

An actor in one of *Morton's* or *Kotzebue's* plays.—MACAULAY.

Putting *Mr. Mill's* and *Mr. Bentham's* principles together. —ID.

397. The possessive preceding the gerund will be considered under the possessive of pronouns (Sec. 408).

PRONOUNS.

PERSONAL PRONOUNS.

I. NOMINATIVE AND OBJECTIVE FORMS.

398. Since most of the personal pronouns, together with the relative *who*, have separate forms for nominative and objective use, there are two general rules that require attention.

> *General rules.*

(1) The *nominative use* is usually marked by the nominative form of the pronoun.

(2) The *objective use* is usually marked by the objective form of the pronoun.

These simple rules are sometimes violated in spoken and in literary English. Some of the violations are universally condemned; others are generally, if not universally, sanctioned.

> *Objective for the nominative.*

399. The objective is sometimes found instead of the nominative in the following instances:—

(1) By a common vulgarism of ignorance or carelessness, no notice is taken of the proper form to be used as subject; as,—

> He and *me* once went in the dead of winter in a one-hoss shay out to Boonville.—WHITCHER, *Bedott Papers*.

> It seems strange to me that *them* that preach up the doctrine don't admire one who carrys it out.—JOSIAH ALLENS WIFE.

(2) By faulty analysis of the sentence, the true relation of the words is misunderstood; for example, "*Whom* think ye that I am?" (In this, *whom* is the complement after the verb *am*, and should be the nominative form, *who*.) "The young Harper, *whom* they agree was rather nice-looking" (*whom* is the subject of the verb *was*).

Especially is this fault to be noticed after an ellipsis with *than* or *as*, the real thought being forgotten; thus,—

> But the consolation coming from devotion did not go far with such a one as *her*.—TROLLOPE.

This should be "as *she*," because the full expression would be "such a one as *she is*."

400. Still, the last expression has the support of many good writers, as shown in the following examples:—

> She was neither better bred nor wiser than you or *me*.—THACKERAY.
>
> No mightier than thyself or *me*.—SHAKESPEARE.
>
> Lin'd with Giants deadlier than *'em* all.—POPE.
>
> But he must be a stronger than *thee*.—SOUTHEY.
>
> Not to render up my soul to such as *thee*.—BYRON.
>
> I shall not learn my duty from such as *thee*.—FIELDING.

A safe rule.

It will be safer for the student to follow the general rule, as illustrated in the following sentences:—

> If so, they are yet holier than *we*.—RUSKIN.
>
> Who would suppose it is the game of such as *he*?—DICKENS.
>
> Do we see
> The robber and the murd'rer weak as *we*?

—MILTON.

I have no other saint than *thou* to pray to.—LONGFELLOW.

> "*Than* whom."

401. One exception is to be noted. The expression **than whom** seems to be used universally instead of "than *who*." There is no special reason for this, but such is the fact; for example,—

>One I remember especially,—one *than whom* I never met a bandit more gallant.—THACKERAY.

>The camp of Richard of England, *than whom* none knows better how to do honor to a noble foe.—SCOTT.

>She had a companion who had been ever agreeable, and her estate a steward *than whom* no one living was supposed to be more competent.—PARTON.

> "*It was* he" *or* "*It was* him"?

402. And there is one question about which grammarians are not agreed, namely, whether the nominative or the objective form should be used in the predicate after *was, is, are,* and the other forms of the verb *be.*

It may be stated with assurance that the literary language *prefers the nominative* in this instance, as,—

>For there was little doubt that it was *he.*—KINGSLEY.

>But still it is not *she.*—MACAULAY.

>And it was *he*
>That made the ship to go.
>—COLERIDGE.

In spoken English, on the other hand, both in England and America, the objective form is regularly found, unless a special, careful effort is made to adopt the standard usage. The following are examples of spoken English from conversations:—

> "Rose Satterne, the mayor's daughter?"—"That's *her*."—KINGSLEY.

> "Who's there?"—"*Me*, Patrick the Porter."—WINTHROP.

> "If there is any one embarrassed, it will not be *me*."—WM. BLACK.

The usage is too common to need further examples.

Exercise.

Correct the italicized pronouns in the following sentences, giving reasons from the analysis of the sentence:—

1. *Whom* they were I really cannot specify.

2. Truth is mightier than *us* all.

3. If there ever was a rogue in the world, it is *me*.

4. They were the very two individuals *whom* we thought were far away.

5. "Seems to me as if *them* as writes must hev a kinder gift fur it, now."

6. The sign of the Good Samaritan is written on the face of *whomsoever* opens to the stranger.

7. It is not *me* you are in love with.

8. You know *whom* it is that you thus charge.

9. The same affinity will exert its influence on *whomsoever* is as noble as these men and women.

10. It was *him* that Horace Walpole called a man who never made a bad figure but as an author.

11. We shall soon see which is the fittest object of scorn, you or *me*.

> *Me* in exclamations.

403. It is to be remembered that the objective form is used in exclamations which turn the attention upon a person; as,—

Unhappy *me!* That I cannot risk my own worthless life.—
KINGSLEY

Alas! miserable *me*! Alas! unhappy Señors!—ID.

Ay *me*! I fondly dream—had ye been there.—MILTON.

> Nominative for the objective.

404. The rule for the objective form is wrongly departed from—

(1) When the object is far removed from the verb, verbal, or preposition which governs it; as, "*He* that can doubt whether he be anything or no, I speak not to" (*he* should be *him*, the object of *to*); "I saw men very like him at each of the places mentioned, but not *he*" (*he* should be *him*, object of *saw*).

(2) In the case of certain pairs of pronouns, used after verbs, verbals, and prepositions, as this from Shakespeare, "All debts are cleared between you and I" (for *you* and *me*); or this, "Let *thou* and *I* the battle try" (for *thee* and *me*, or *us*).

(3) By forgetting the construction, in the case of words used in apposition with the object; as, "Ask the murderer, *he* who has steeped his hands in the blood of another" (instead of "*him* who," the word being in apposition with *murderer*).

> *Exception 1*, who *interrogative*.

405. The interrogative pronoun **who** may be said to have no objective form in spoken English. We regularly say, "*Who* did you see?" or, "*Who* were they talking to?" etc. The more formal "To *whom* were they talking?" sounds stilted in conversation, and is usually avoided.

> Knows he now to *whom* he lies under obligation?—SCOTT.
>
> What doth she look on? *Whom* doth she behold?—WORDSWORTH.

Yet the nominative form is found quite frequently to divide the work of the objective use; for example,—

> My son is going to be married to I don't know *who*.—GOLDSMITH.
>
> *Who* have we here?—ID.
>
> *Who* should I meet the other day but my old friend.—STEELE.
>
> He hath given away half his fortune to the Lord knows *who*.—KINGSLEY.
>
> *Who* have we got here?—SMOLLETT.
>
> *Who* should we find there but Eustache?—MARRVAT.
>
> *Who* the devil is he talking to?—SHERIDAN.

Exception 2, but he, *etc.*

406. It is a well-established usage to put the nominative form, as well as the objective, after the preposition *but* (sometimes *save*); as,—

> All were knocked down but *us* two.—KINGSLEY.
>
> Thy shores are empires, changed in all save *thee*.—BYRON.
>
> Rich are the sea gods:—who gives gifts but *they?*—EMERSON.
>
>   The Chieftains then
> Returned rejoicing, all but *he*.
> —SOUTHEY
>
> No man strikes him but *I*.—KINGSLEY.
>
> None, save *thou* and thine, I've sworn,

Shall be left upon the morn.
—BYRON.

Exercise.

Correct the italicized pronouns in the following, giving reasons from the analysis of the quotation:—

1. *Thou*, Nature, partial Nature, I arraign.

2. Let you and *I* look at these, for they say there are none such in the world.

3. "Nonsense!" said Amyas, "we could kill every soul of them in half an hour, and they know that as well as *me*."

4. Markland, *who*, with Jortin and Thirlby, Johnson calls three contemporaries of great eminence.

5. They are coming for a visit to *she* and *I*.

6.

    They crowned him long ago;
But *who* they got to put it on
    Nobody seems to know.

7. I experienced little difficulty in distinguishing among the pedestrians *they* who had business with St. Bartholomew.

8. The great difference lies between the laborer who moves to Yorkshire and *he* who moves to Canada.

9. Besides my father and Uncle Haddock—*he* of the silver plates.

10.

Ye against whose familiar names not yet
The fatal asterisk of death is set,
Ye I salute.

11. It can't be worth much to *they* that hasn't larning.

12. To send me away for a whole year—*I* who had never crept from under the parental wing—was a startling idea.

II. POSSESSIVE FORMS.

> *As antecedent of a relative.*

407. The possessive forms of personal pronouns and also of nouns are sometimes found as antecedents of relatives. This usage is not frequent. The antecedent is usually nominative or objective, as the use of the possessive is less likely to be clear.

> We should augur ill of any *gentleman's* property to whom this happened every other day in his drawing room.—RUSKIN.

> For *their* sakes whose distance disabled them from knowing me.—C. B. BROWN.

> Now by *His* name that I most reverence in Heaven, and by *hers* whom I most worship on earth.—SCOTT.

> He saw her smile and slip money into the *man's* hand who was ordered to ride behind the coach.—THACKERAY.

> He doubted whether *his* signature whose expectations were so much more bounded would avail.—DE QUINCEY.

> For boys with hearts as bold
> As *his* who kept the bridge so well.
> —MACAULAY.

> *Preceding a gerund,—possessive, or objective?*

408. Another point on which there is some variance in usage is such a construction as this: "We heard of *Brown* studying law," or "We heard of *Brown's* studying law."

That is, should the possessive case of a noun or pronoun always be used with the gerund to indicate the active agent? Closely scrutinizing these two sentences quoted, we might find a difference between them: saying that in the first one *studying* is a participle, and the meaning is, *We heard of Brown,* [who was] *studying law;* and that in the second, *studying* is a gerund, object of *heard of,* and modified by the possessive case as any other substantive would be.

> *Why both are found.*

But in common use there is no such distinction. Both types of sentences are found; both are gerunds; sometimes the gerund has the possessive form before it, sometimes it has the objective. The use of the objective is older, and in keeping with the old way of regarding the *person* as the chief object before the mind: the possessive use is more modern, in keeping with the disposition to proceed from the material thing to the *abstract idea*, and to make the action substantive the chief idea before the mind.

In the examples quoted, it will be noticed that the possessive of the pronoun is more common than that of the noun.

> *Objective.*

    The last incident which I recollect, was my learned and worthy *patron* falling from a chair.—SCOTT.

    He spoke of *some one* coming to drink tea with him, and asked why it was not made.—THACKERAY.

    The old sexton even expressed a doubt as to *Shakespeare* having been born in her house.—IRVING.

    The fact of the *Romans* not burying their dead within the city walls proper is a strong reason, etc.—BREWER.

    I remember *Wordsworth* once laughingly reporting to me a little personal anecdote.—DE QUINCEY.

    Here I state them only in brief, to prevent the *reader* casting about in alarm for my ultimate meaning.—RUSKIN.

We think with far less pleasure of *Cato* tearing out his entrails than of *Russell* saying, as he turned away from his wife, that the bitterness of death was past.—Macaulay.

There is actually a kind of sacredness in the fact of such a *man* being sent into this earth.—Carlyle.

> *Possessive.*

There is no use for any *man's* taking up his abode in a house built of glass.—Carlyle.

As to *his* having good grounds on which to rest an action for life.—Dickens.

The case was made known to me by a *man's* holding out the little creature dead.—De Quincey.

There may be reason for a *savage's* preferring many kinds of food which the civilized man rejects.—Thoreau.

It informs me of the previous circumstances of *my* laying aside my clothes.—C. Brockden Brown.

The two strangers gave me an account of *their* once having been themselves in a somewhat similar condition.—Audubon.

There was a chance of *their* being sent to a new school, where there were examinations.—Ruskin

This can only be by *his* preferring truth to his past apprehension of truth.—Emerson

III. PERSONAL PRONOUNS AND THEIR ANTECEDENTS.

409. The pronouns of the third person usually refer back to some preceding noun or pronoun, and ought to agree with them in person, number, and gender.

> *Watch for the real antecedent.*

There are two constructions in which the student will need to watch the pronoun,—when the antecedent, in one person, is followed by a phrase containing a pronoun of a different person; and when the antecedent is of such a form that the pronoun following cannot indicate exactly the gender. Examples of these constructions are,—

> *Those* of us who can only maintain *themselves* by continuing in some business or salaried office.—RUSKIN.
>
> Suppose the life and fortune of *every one* of us would depend on *his* winning or losing a game of chess.—HUXLEY.
>
> If *any one* did not know it, it was *his* own fault.—CABLE.
>
> *Everybody* had *his* own life to think of.—DEFOE.

410. In such a case as the last three sentences,—when the antecedent includes both masculine and feminine, or is a distributive word, taking in each of many persons,—the preferred method is to put the pronoun following in the masculine singular; if the antecedent is neuter, preceded by a distributive, the pronoun will be neuter singular.

The following are additional examples:—

> The next *correspondent* wants you to mark out a whole course of life for *him*.—HOLMES.
>
> Every *city* threw open *its* gates.—DE QUINCEY.
>
> Every *person* who turns this page has *his* own little diary.—THACKERAY.
>
> The pale realms of shade, where *each* shall take
> *His* chamber in the silent halls of death.
> —BRYANT.

> *Avoided: By using both pronouns.*

Sometimes this is avoided by using both the masculine and the feminine pronoun; for example,—

Not the feeblest *grandame*, not a mowing *idiot*, but uses what spark of perception and faculty is left, to chuckle and triumph in *his or her* opinion.—EMERSON.

It is a game which has been played for untold ages, every *man* and *woman* of us being one of the two players in a game of *his or her* own.—HUXLEY.

By using the plural pronoun.

411. Another way of referring to an antecedent which is a distributive pronoun or a noun modified by a distributive adjective, is to use the plural of the pronoun following. This is not considered the best usage, the logical analysis requiring the singular pronoun in each case; but the construction is frequently found *when the antecedent includes or implies both genders*. The masculine does not really represent a feminine antecedent, and the expression *his or her* is avoided as being cumbrous.

Notice the following examples of the plural:—

Neither of the sisters *were* very much deceived.—THACKERAY.

Every one must judge of *their* own feelings.—BYRON.

Had the doctor been contented to take my dining tables, as *anybody* in *their* senses would have done.—AUSTEN.

If the part deserve any comment, every considering *Christian* will make it *themselves* as they go.—DEFOE.

Every person's happiness depends in part upon the respect *they* meet in the world.—PALEY.

Every nation have *their* refinements—STERNE.

Neither gave vent to *their* feelings in words.—SCOTT.

Each of the nations acted according to *their* national custom.—PALGRAVE.

The sun, which pleases *everybody* with it and with *themselves*.—RUSKIN.

Urging *every one* within reach of your influence to be neat, and giving *them* means of being so.—Iᴅ.

Everybody will become of use in *their* own fittest way.—Iᴅ.

Everybody said *they* thought it was the newest thing there.—Wᴇɴᴅᴇʟʟ Pʜɪʟʟɪᴘꜱ.

Struggling for life, *each* almost bursting *their* sinews to force the other off.—Pᴀᴜʟᴅɪɴɢ.

Whosoever hath any gold, let *them* break it off.—Bɪʙʟᴇ.

Nobody knows what it is to lose a friend, till *they* have lost him.—Fɪᴇʟᴅɪɴɢ.

Where she was gone, or what was become of her, *no one* could take upon *them* to say.—Sʜᴇʀɪᴅᴀɴ.

I do not mean that I think *any one* to blame for taking due care of *their* health.—Aᴅᴅɪꜱᴏɴ.

Exercise.—In the above sentences, *unless both genders are implied*, change the pronoun to agree with its antecedent.

RELATIVE PRONOUNS.

I. RESTRICTIVE AND UNRESTRICTIVE RELATIVES.

> *What these terms mean.*

412. As to their conjunctive use, the definite relatives **who**, **which**, and **that** may be **coördinating** or **restrictive**.

A relative, when coördinating, or unrestrictive, is equivalent to a conjunction (*and, but, because,* etc.) and a personal pronoun. It adds a new statement to what precedes, that being considered already clear; as, "I gave it to the beggar, *who* went away." This means, "I gave it to the beggar [we know which one], *and he* went away."

A relative, when restrictive, introduces a clause to limit and make clear some preceding word. The clause is restricted to the antecedent, and does not add a new statement; it merely couples a thought necessary to define the antecedent: as, "I gave it to a beggar *who* stood at the gate." It defines *beggar*.

413. It is sometimes contended that **who** and **which** should always be coördinating, and **that** always restrictive; but, according to the practice of every modern writer, the usage must be stated as follows:—

> *A loose rule the only one to be formulated.*

Who and **which** are either coördinating or restrictive, the taste of the writer and regard for euphony being the guide.

That is in most cases restrictive, the coördinating use not being often found among careful writers.

Exercise.

In the following examples, tell whether *who*, *which*, and *that* are restrictive or not, in each instance:—

> Who.

1. "Here he is now!" cried those who stood near Ernest.—HAWTHORNE.

2. He could overhear the remarks of various individuals, who were comparing the features with the face on the mountain side.—ID.

3. The particular recording angel who heard it pretended not to understand, or it might have gone hard with the tutor.—HOLMES.

4. Yet how many are there who up, down, and over England are saying, etc.—H. W. BEECHER

5. A grizzly-looking man appeared, whom we took to be sixty or seventy years old.—THOREAU.

> Which.

6. The volume which I am just about terminating is almost as much English history as Dutch.—MOTLEY.

7. On hearing their plan, which was to go over the Cordilleras, she agreed to join the party.—DE QUINCEY.

8. Even the wild story of the incident which had immediately occasioned the explosion of this madness fell in with the universal prostration of mind.—ID.

9. Their colloquies are all gone to the fire except this first, which Mr. Hare has printed.—CARLYLE.

10. There is a particular science which takes these matters in hand, and it is called logic.—NEWMAN.

> That.

11. So different from the wild, hard-mouthed horses at Westport, that were often vicious.—DE QUINCEY.

12. He was often tempted to pluck the flowers that rose everywhere about him in the greatest variety.—ADDISON.

13. He felt a gale of perfumes breathing upon him, that grew stronger and sweeter in proportion as he advanced.—ID.

14. With narrow shoulders, long arms and legs, hands that dangled a mile out of his sleeves.—IRVING.

II. RELATIVE AND ANTECEDENT.

> The rule.

414. The general rule is, that the relative pronoun agrees with its antecedent in person and number.

> *In what sense true.*

This cannot be true as to the form of the pronoun, as that does not vary for person or number. We say *I, you, he, they*, etc., *who; these* or *that which*, etc. However, the relative *carries over* the agreement from the antecedent before to the verb following, so far as the verb has forms to show its agreement with a substantive. For example, in the sentence, "He that writes to himself writes to an eternal public," *that* is invariable as to person and number, but, because of its antecedent, it makes the verb third person singular.

Notice the agreement in the following sentences:—

> There is not *one* of the company, but *myself*, who rarely *speak* at all, but *speaks* of him as that sort, etc.—ADDISON.
>
> O *Time!* who *know'st* a lenient hand to lay Softest on sorrow's wound.—BOWLES.
>
> Let us be of good cheer, remembering that the misfortunes hardest to bear are *those* which never *come*.—LOWELL.

> *A disputed point.*

415. This prepares the way for the consideration of one of the vexed questions,—whether we should say, "one of the finest books that *has* been published," or, "one of the finest books that *have* been published."

> One of ... [*plural*] that who, *or* which ... [*singular or plural*.]

Both constructions are frequently found, the reason being a difference of opinion as to the antecedent. Some consider it to be *one* [book] *of the finest books*, with *one* as the principal word, the true antecedent; others regard *books* as the antecedent, and write the verb in the plural. The latter is rather more frequent, but the former has good authority.

The following quotations show both sides:—

> *Plural.*

He was one of the very few commanders who *appear* to have shown equal skill in directing a campaign, in winning a battle, and in improving a victory.—LECKY.

He was one of the most distinguished scientists who *have* ever lived.—J. T. MORSE, JR., *Franklin.*

It is one of those periods which *shine* with an unnatural and delusive splendor.—MACAULAY.

A very little encouragement brought back one of those overflows which *make* one more ashamed, etc.—HOLMES.

I am one of those who *believe* that the real will never find an irremovable basis till it rests on the ideal.—LOWELL.

French literature of the eighteenth century, one of the most powerful agencies that *have* ever existed.—M. ARNOLD.

What man's life is not overtaken by one or more of those tornadoes that *send* us out of our course?—THACKERAY.

He is one of those that *deserve* very well.—ADDISON.

> *Singular.*

The fiery youth ... struck down one of those who *was* pressing hardest.—SCOTT.

He appeared to me one of the noblest creatures that ever *was*, when he derided the shams of society.—HOWELLS.

A rare Roundabout performance,—one of the very best that *has* ever appeared in this series.—THACKERAY.

Valancourt was the hero of one of the most famous romances which ever *was* published in this country.—ID.

It is one of the errors which *has* been diligently propagated by designing writers.—IRVING.

"I am going to breakfast with one of these fellows who *is* at the Piazza Hotel."—DICKENS.

The "Economy of the Animal Kingdom" is one of those books which *is* an honor to the human race.—EMERSON.

Tom Puzzle is one of the most eminent immethodical disputants of any that *has* fallen under my observation.—ADDISON.

The richly canopied monument of one of the most earnest souls that ever gave *itself* to the arts.—RUSKIN.

III. OMISSION OF THE RELATIVE.

416. Although the omission of the relative is common when it would be the object of the verb or preposition *expressed*, there is an omission which is not frequently found in careful writers; that is, when the relative word is a pronoun, object of a preposition *understood*, or is equivalent to the conjunction *when, where, whence,* and such like: as, "He returned by the same route [by which] he came;" "India is the place [in which, or where] he died." Notice these sentences:—

In the posture I lay, I could see nothing except the sky.—SWIFT.

This is he that should marshal us the way we were going.—
EMERSON.

But I by backward steps would move;
And, when this dust falls to the urn,
In that same state I came, return.
—VAUGHAN.

Welcome the hour my aged limbs
Are laid with thee to rest.
—BURNS.

The night was concluded in the manner we began the morning.
—Goldsmith.

The same day I went aboard we set sail.—Defoe.

The vulgar historian of a Cromwell fancies that he had determined on being Protector of England, at the time he was plowing the marsh lands of Cambridgeshire.—Carlyle.

To pass under the canvas in the manner he had entered required time and attention.—Scott.

Exercise.—In the above sentences, insert the omitted conjunction or phrase, and see if the sentence is made clearer.

IV. THE RELATIVE *AS* AFTER *SAME*.

417. It is very rarely that we find such sentences as,—

He considered...me as his apprentice, and accordingly expected the same service from me *as* he would from another.—Franklin.

This has the same effect in natural faults *as* maiming and mutilation produce from accidents.—Burke.

> *The regular construction.*

> *Caution.*

The usual way is to use the relative *as* after *same* if no verb follows *as;* but, if *same* is followed by a complete clause, *as* is not used, but we find the relative *who, which,* or *that.* Remember this applies only to *as* when used as a relative.

Examples of the use of *as* in a contracted clause:—

Looking to the same end *as* Turner, and working in the same spirit, he, with Turner, was a discoverer, etc.—R. W. Church.

They believe the same of all the works of art, *as* of knives, boats, looking-glasses.—Addison.

Examples of relatives following *same* in full clauses:—

> Who.

This is the very same rogue *who* sold us the spectacles. — Goldsmith.

The same person *who* had clapped his thrilling hands at the first representation of the Tempest.—Macaulay.

> That.

I rubbed on some of the same ointment *that* was given me at my first arrival.—Swift.

> Which.

For the same sound is in my ears
Which in those days I heard.
—Wordsworth.

With the same minuteness *which* her predecessor had exhibited, she passed the lamp over her face and person.—Scott.

V. MISUSE OF RELATIVE PRONOUNS.

> *Anacoluthic use of* which.

418. There is now and then found in the pages of literature a construction which imitates the Latin, but which is usually carefully avoided. It is a use of the relative *which* so as to make an anacoluthon, or lack of proper connection between the clauses; for example,—

Which, if I had resolved to go on with, I might as well have staid at home.—Defoe

Which if he attempted to do, Mr. Billings vowed that he would follow him to Jerusalem.—THACKERAY.

We know not the incantation of the heart that would wake them; —*which* if they once heard, they would start up to meet us in the power of long ago.—RUSKIN.

He delivered the letter, *which* when Mr. Thornhill had read, he said that all submission was now too late.—GOLDSMITH.

But still the house affairs would draw her thence;
Which ever as she could with haste dispatch,
She'd come again.
—SHAKESPEARE.

As the sentences stand, *which* really has no office in the sentence: it should be changed to a demonstrative or a personal pronoun, and this be placed in the proper clause.

Exercise.—Rewrite the above five sentences so as to make the proper grammatical connection in each.

> And who, and which, *etc.*

419. There is another kind of expression which slips into the lines of even standard authors, but which is always regarded as an oversight and a blemish.

The following sentence affords an example: "The rich are now engaged in distributing what remains among the poorer sort, *and who* are now thrown upon their compassion." The trouble is that such conjunctions as *and, but, or*, etc., should connect expressions of the same kind: *and who* makes us look for a preceding *who*, but none is expressed. There are three ways to remedy the sentence quoted: thus, (1) "Among those *who* are poor, *and who* are now," etc.; (2) "Among the poorer sort, *who* are now thrown," etc.; (3) "Among the poorer sort, now thrown upon their," etc. That is,—

> *Direction for rewriting.*

Express both relatives, or omit the conjunction, or leave out both connective and relative.

Exercise.

Rewrite the following examples according to the direction just given:—

> And who.

1. Hester bestowed all her means on wretches less miserable than herself, and who not unfrequently insulted the hand that fed them.—HAWTHORNE.

2. With an albatross perched on his shoulder, and who might be introduced to the congregation as the immediate organ of his conversion.—DE QUINCEY.

3. After this came Elizabeth herself, then in the full glow of what in a sovereign was called beauty, and who would in the lowest walk of life have been truly judged to possess a noble figure.—SCOTT.

4. This was a gentleman, once a great favorite of M. le Conte, and in whom I myself was not a little interested.—THACKERAY.

> But who.

5. Yonder woman was the wife of a certain learned man, English by name, but who had long dwelt in Amsterdam.—HAWTHORNE.

6. Dr. Ferguson considered him as a man of a powerful capacity, but whose mind was thrown off its just bias.—SCOTT.

> Or who.

7. "What knight so craven, then," exclaims the chivalrous Venetian, "that he would not have been more than a match for the stoutest adversary; or who would not have lost his life a

thousand times sooner than return dishonored by the lady of his love?"—PRESCOTT.

> And which.

8. There are peculiar quavers still to be heard in that church, and which may even be heard a mile off.—IRVING.

9. The old British tongue was replaced by a debased Latin, like that spoken in the towns, and in which inscriptions are found in the western counties.—PEARSON.

10. I shall have complete copies, one of signal interest, and which has never been described.—MOTLEY.

> But which.

11. "A mockery, indeed, but in which the soul trifled with itself!"—HAWTHORNE.

12. I saw upon the left a scene far different, but which yet the power of dreams had reconciled into harmony.—DE QUINCEY.

> Or which.

13. He accounted the fair-spoken courtesy, which the Scotch had learned, either from imitation of their frequent allies, the French, or which might have arisen from their own proud and reserved character, as a false and astucious mark, etc.—SCOTT.

> That ... and which, *etc.*

420. Akin to the above is another fault, which is likewise a variation from the best usage. Two different relatives are sometimes found referring back to the same antecedent in one sentence; whereas the better practice is to choose one relative, and repeat this for any further reference.

Exercise.

Rewrite the following quotations by repeating one relative instead of using two for the same antecedent:—

> That ... who.

1. Still in the confidence of children that tread without fear every chamber in their father's house, and to whom no door is closed.—DE QUINCEY.

2. Those renowned men that were our ancestors as much as yours, and whose examples and principles we inherit.—BEECHER.

3. The Tree Igdrasil, that has its roots down in the kingdoms of Hela and Death, and whose boughs overspread the highest heaven!—CARLYLE.

> That ... which.

4. Christianity is a religion that reveals men as the object of God's infinite love, and which commends him to the unbounded love of his brethren.—W. E. CHANNING.

5. He flung into literature, in his Mephistopheles, the first organic figure that has been added for some ages, and which will remain as long as the Prometheus.—EMERSON.

6. Gutenburg might also have struck out an idea that surely did not require any extraordinary ingenuity, and which left the most important difficulties to be surmounted.—HALLAM.

7. Do me the justice to tell me what I have a title to be acquainted with, and which I am certain to know more truly from you than from others.—SCOTT.

8. He will do this amiable little service out of what one may say old civilization has established in place of goodness of heart, but which is perhaps not so different from it.—HOWELLS.

9. In my native town of Salem, at the head of what, half a century ago, was a bustling wharf,—but which is now burdened with decayed wooden warehouses.—HAWTHORNE.

10. His recollection of what he considered as extreme presumption in the Knight of the Leopard, even when he stood high in the roles of chivalry, but which, in his present condition, appeared an insult sufficient to drive the fiery monarch into a frenzy of passion.—SCOTT

> That which ... what.

11. He, now without any effort but that which he derived from the sill, and what little his feet could secure the irregular crevices, was hung in air.—W. G. SIMMS.

> Such as ... which.

12. It rose into a thrilling passion, such as my heart had always dimly craved and hungered after, but which now first interpreted itself to my ear.—DE QUINCEY.

13. I recommend some honest manual calling, such as they have very probably been bred to, and which will at least give them a chance of becoming President.—HOLMES.

> Such as ... whom.

14. I grudge the dollar, the dime, the cent, I give to such men as do not belong to me, and to whom I do not belong.—EMERSON.

> Which ... that ... that.

15. That evil influence which carried me first away from my father's house, that hurried me into the wild and undigested notion of making my fortune, and that impressed these conceits so forcibly upon me.—DEFOE.

ADJECTIVE PRONOUNS.

> Each other, one another.

421. The student is sometimes troubled whether to use **each other** or **one another** in expressing reciprocal relation or action. Whether either one refers to a certain number of persons or objects, whether or not the two are equivalent, may be gathered from a study of the following sentences:—

> They [Ernest and the poet] led *one another*, as it were, into the high pavilion of their thoughts.—HAWTHORNE.
>
> Men take *each other's* measure when they meet for the first time.—EMERSON.
>
> You ruffian! do you fancy I forget that we were fond of *each other*?—THACKERAY.
>
> England was then divided between kings and Druids, always at war with *one another*, carrying off *each other's* cattle and wives.—BREWER
>
> The topics follow *each other* in the happiest order.—MACAULAY.
>
> The Peers at a conference begin to pommel *each other*.—ID.
>
> We call ourselves a rich nation, and we are filthy and foolish enough to thumb *each other's* books out of circulating libraries.—RUSKIN.
>
> The real hardships of life are now coming fast upon us; let us not increase them by dissension among *each other*.—GOLDSMITH.
>
> In a moment we were all shaking hands with *one another*.—DICKENS.
>
> The unjust purchaser forces the two to bid against *each other*.—RUSKIN.

> *Distributives* either *and* neither.

422. By their original meaning, **either** and **neither** refer to only two persons or objects; as, for example,—

> Some one must be poor, and in want of his gold—or his corn. Assume that no one is in want of *either*.—RUSKIN
>
> Their [Ernest's and the poet's] minds accorded into one strain, and made delightful music which *neither* could have claimed as all his own.—HAWTHORNE.

Use of any.

Sometimes these are made to refer to several objects, in which case any should be used instead; as,—

> Was it the winter's storm? was it hard labor and spare meals? was it disease? was it the tomahawk? Is it possible that *neither* of these causes, that not all combined, were able to blast this bud of hope?—EVERETT.
>
> Once I took such delight in Montaigne ...; before that, in Shakespeare; then in Plutarch; then in Plotinus; at one time in Bacon; afterwards in Goethe; even in Bettine; but now I turn the pages of *either* of them languidly, whilst I still cherish their genius.—EMERSON.

Any *usually plural.*

423. The adjective pronoun **any** is nearly always regarded as plural, as shown in the following sentences:—

> If *any* of you *have* been accustomed to look upon these hours as mere visionary hours, I beseech you, etc.—BEECHER
>
> Whenever, during his stay at Yuste, *any* of his friends had died, he had been punctual in doing honor to *their* memory.—STIRLING.

But I enjoy the company and conversation of its inhabitants, when *any* of them *are* so good as to visit me.—FRANKLIN.

Do you think, when I spoke anon of the ghosts of Pryor's children, I mean that *any* of them *are* dead?—THACKERAY.

In earlier Modern English, *any* was often singular; as,—

If *any*, speak; for *him* have I offended.—SHAKESPEARE.

If *any* of you lack wisdom, let *him* ask of God.—*BIBLE*.

Very rarely the singular is met with in later times; as,—

Here is a poet doubtless as much affected by his own descriptions as *any* that *reads* them can be.—BURKE.

> *Caution.*

The above instances are to be distinguished from the adjective *any*, which is plural as often as singular.

> None *usually plural.*

424. The adjective pronoun **none** is, in the prose of the present day, usually plural, although it is historically a contraction of *ne ān* (not one). Examples of its use are,—

In earnest, if ever man was; as *none* of the French philosophers *were*.—CARLYLE.

None of Nature's powers *do* better service.—PROF. DANA

One man answers some question which *none* of his contemporaries *put*, and is isolated.—EMERSON.

None obey the command of duty so well as those who are free from the observance of slavish bondage.—SCOTT.

Do you think, when I spoke anon of the ghosts of Pryor's children, I mean that any of them are dead? *None are*, that I know of.—THACKERAY.

Early apples begin to be ripe about the first of August; but I think *none* of them *are* so good to eat as some to smell.—THOREAU.

The singular use of *none* is often found in the Bible; as,—

None of them *was* cleansed, saving Naaman the Syrian.—LUKE IV 27

Also the singular is sometimes found in present-day English in prose, and less rarely in poetry; for example,—

> Perhaps *none* of our Presidents since Washington *has* stood so firm in the confidence of the people.—LOWELL
>
> In signal *none his* steed should spare.—SCOTT

Like the use of *any*, the pronoun *none* should be distinguished from the adjective *none,* which is used absolutely, and hence is more likely to confuse the student.

Compare with the above the following sentences having the adjective *none*:—

> Reflecting a summer evening sky in its bosom, though *none* [no sky] was visible overhead.—THOREAU
>
> The holy fires were suffered to go out in the temples, and *none* [no fires] were lighted in their own dwellings.—PRESCOTT

All *singular and plural.*

---

425. The pronoun **all** has the singular construction when it means *everything*; the plural, when it means *all persons*: for example,—

Singular.

> The light troops thought ... that *all was* lost.—PALGRAVE
>
> *All was* won on the one side, and *all was* lost on the other.—BAYNE
>
> Having done *all* that *was* just toward others.—NAPIER

Plural.

> But the King's treatment of the great lords will be judged leniently by *all* who *remember*, etc.—PEARSON.
>
> When *all were* gone, fixing his eyes on the mace, etc.—LINGARD

All who did not understand French *were* compelled, etc.—MCMASTER.

> Somebody's else, *or* somebody else's?

426. The compounds **somebody else, any one else, nobody else**, etc., are treated as units, and the apostrophe is regularly added to the final word *else* instead of the first. Thackeray has the expression *somebody's else*, and Ford has *nobody's else*, but the regular usage is shown in the following selections:—

A boy who is fond of *somebody else's* pencil case.—G. ELIOT.

A suit of clothes like *somebody else's*.—THACKERAY.

Drawing off his gloves and warming his hands before the fire as benevolently as if they were *somebody else's*.—DICKENS.

Certainly not! nor *any one else's* ropes.—RUSKIN.

Again, my pronunciation—like *everyone else's*—is in some cases more archaic.—SWEET.

Then everybody wanted some of *somebody else's*.—RUSKIN.

His hair...curled once all over it in long tendrils, unlike *anybody else's* in the world.—N. P. WILLIS.

"Ye see, there ain't nothin' wakes folks up like *somebody else's* wantin' what you've got."—MRS. STOWE.

ADJECTIVES.

AGREEMENT OF ADJECTIVES WITH NOUNS.

> These sort, all manner of, *etc.*

427. The statement that adjectives agree with their nouns in number is restricted to the words **this** and **that** (with **these** and **those**), as these are the only adjectives that have separate forms for singular and plural; and it is only in one set of expressions that the concord seems to be violated,—in such as "*these sort* of books," "*those kind* of trees," "*all manner* of men;" the nouns being singular, the adjectives plural. These expressions are all but universal in spoken English, and may be found not infrequently in literary English; for example,—

These kind of knaves I know, which in this plainness
Harbor more craft, etc.
—SHAKESPEARE

All *these sort* of things.—SHERIDAN.

I hoped we had done with *those sort* of things.—MULOCH.

You have been so used to *those sort* of impertinences.SYDNEY SMITH.

Whitefield or Wesley, or some other such great man as a bishop, or *those sort* of people.—FIELDING.

I always delight in overthrowing *those kind* of schemes.—AUSTEN.

There are women as well as men who can thoroughly enjoy *those sort* of romantic spots.—*Saturday Review*, London.

The library was open, with *all manner* of amusing books.—
Ruskin.

According to the approved usage of Modern English, each one of the above adjectives would have to be changed to the singular, or the nouns to the plural.

> *History of this construction.*

The reason for the prevalence of these expressions must be sought in the history of the language: it cannot be found in the statement that the adjective is made plural by the attraction of a noun following.

> *At the source.*

In Old and Middle English, in keeping with the custom of looking at things concretely rather than in the abstract, they said, not "all *kinds* of wild animals," but "alles cunnes wilde deor" (wild animals of-every-kind). This the modern expression reverses.

> *Later form.*

But in early Middle English the modern way of regarding such expressions also appeared, gradually displacing the old.

> *The result.*

Consequently we have a confused expression. We keep the form of logical agreement in standard English, such as, "*This sort* of trees should be planted;" but at the same time the noun following *kind of* is felt to be the real subject, and the adjective is, in spoken English, made to agree with it, which accounts for the construction, "*These kind of* trees are best."

> *A question.*

The inconvenience of the logical construction is seen when we wish to use a predicate with number forms. Should we say, "This kind of rules *are* the best," or "This kind of rules *is* the best?" *Kind* or *sort* may be treated as a collective noun, and in this way may take a plural verb; for example,

Burke's sentence, "A *sort* of uncertain sounds *are*, when the necessary dispositions concur, more alarming than a total silence."

COMPARATIVE AND SUPERLATIVE FORMS.

Use of the comparative degree.

428. The comparative degree of the adjective (or adverb) is used when we wish to compare two objects or sets of objects, or one object with a class of objects, to express a higher degree of quality; as,—

> Which is *the better* able to defend himself,—a strong man with nothing but his fists, or a paralytic cripple encumbered with a sword which he cannot lift?—MACAULAY.

> Of two such lessons, why forget
>   The *nobler* and the *manlier* one?
> —BYRON.

> We may well doubt which has the *stronger* claim to civilization, the victor or the vanquished.—PRESCOTT.

> A *braver* ne'er to battle rode.—SCOTT.

> He is *taller,* by almost the breadth of my nail, than any of his court.—SWIFT.

Other after the comparative form.

429. When an object is compared with the class to which it belongs, it is regularly excluded from that class by the word *other*; if not, the object would really be compared with itself: thus,—

> The character of Lady Castlewood has required more delicacy in its manipulation than perhaps any *other* which Thackeray has drawn.—TROLLOPE.

> I used to watch this patriarchal personage with livelier curiosity than any *other* form of humanity.—HAWTHORNE.

Exercise.

See if the word *other* should be inserted in the following sentences:—

1. There was no man who could make a more graceful bow than Mr. Henry.—Wirt.

2. I am concerned to see that Mr. Gary, to whom Dante owes more than ever poet owed to translator, has sanctioned, etc.—Macaulay.

3. There is no country in which wealth is so sensible of its obligations as our own.—Lowell.

4. This is more sincerely done in the Scandinavian than in any mythology I know.—Carlyle.

5. In "Thaddeus of Warsaw" there is more crying than in any novel I remember to have read.—Thackeray.

6. The heroes of another writer [Cooper] are quite the equals of Scott's men; perhaps Leather-stocking is better than any one in "Scott's lot."—Id.

Use of the superlative degree.

430. The **superlative degree** of the adjective (or adverb) is used regularly in comparing more than two things, but is also frequently used in comparing only two things.

Examples of superlative with several objects:—

It is a case of which the *simplest* statement is the *strongest*.—Macaulay.

Even Dodd himself, who was one of the *greatest* humbugs who ever lived, would not have had the face.—Thackeray.

To the man who plays well, the *highest* stakes are paid.—Huxley.

> *Superlative with two objects.*

Compare the first three sentences in Sec. 428 with the following:—

> Which do you love *best* to behold, the lamb or the lion? — THACKERAY.

> Which of these methods has the *best* effect? Both of them are the same to the sense, and differ only in form.—DR BLAIR.

> Rip was one of those ... who eat white bread or brown, whichever can be got *easiest*.—IRVING.

> It is hard to say whether the man of wisdom or the man of folly contributed *most* to the amusement of the party.—SCOTT.

> There was an interval of three years between Mary and Anne. The *eldest*, Mary, was like the Stuarts—the *younger* was a fair English child.—MRS. OLIPHANT.

> Of the two great parties which at this hour almost share the nation between them, I should say that one has the *best* cause, and the other contains the *best* men.—EMERSON.

> In all disputes between States, though the *strongest* is nearly always mainly in the wrong, the *weaker* is often so in a minor degree.—RUSKIN.

> She thought him and Olivia extremely of a size, and would bid both to stand up to see which was the *tallest*.—GOLDSMITH.

> These two properties seem essential to wit, more particularly the *last* of them.—ADDISON.

> "Ha, ha, ha!" roared Goodman Brown when the wind laughed at him. "Let us see which will laugh *loudest*."—HAWTHORNE.

> *Double comparative and superlative.*

431. In Shakespeare's time it was quite common to use a double comparative and superlative by using *more* or *most* before the word already

having *-er* or *-est*. Examples from Shakespeare are,—

> How much *more elder* art thou than thy looks!—*Merchant of Venice.*
>
> Nor that I am *more better* than Prospero.—Tᴇᴍᴘᴇsᴛ.
>
> Come you *more nearer.*—Hᴀᴍʟᴇᴛ.
>
> With the *most boldest* and best hearts of Rome.—*J.* Cᴀᴇsᴀʀ.

Also from the same period,—

> Imitating the manner of the *most ancientest* and *finest* Grecians.—Bᴇɴ Jᴏɴsᴏɴ.
>
> After the *most straitest* sect of our religion.—*Bible,* 1611.

Such expressions are now heard only in vulgar English. The following examples are used purposely, to represent the characters as ignorant persons:—

> The artful saddler persuaded the young traveler to look at "the *most convenientest* and *handsomest* saddle that ever was seen."—Bᴜʟᴡᴇʀ.
>
> "There's nothing comes out but the *most lowest* stuff in nature; not a bit of high life among them."—Gᴏʟᴅsᴍɪᴛʜ.

THREE FIRST **OR** *FIRST THREE?*

432. As to these two expressions, over which a little war has so long been buzzing, we think it not necessary to say more than that both are in good use; not only so in popular speech, but in literary English. Instances of both are given below.

The meaning intended is the same, and the reader gets the same idea from both: hence there is properly a perfect liberty in the use of either or both.

> First three, *etc.*

For Carlyle, and Secretary Walsingham also, have been helping them heart and soul for the *last two* years.—KINGSLEY.

The delay in the *first three* lines, and conceit in the last, jar upon us constantly.—RUSKIN.

The *last dozen* miles before you reach the suburbs.—DE QUINCEY.

Mankind for the *first seventy thousand* ages ate their meat raw.—LAMB.

The *first twenty* numbers were expressed by a corresponding number of dots. The *first five* had specific names.—PRESCOTT.

> Three first, *etc.*

These are the *three first* needs of civilized life.—RUSKIN.

He has already finished the *three first* sticks of it.—ADDISON.

In my *two last* you had so much of Lismahago that I suppose you are glad he is gone.—SMOLLETT.

I have not numbered the lines except of the *four first* books. — COWPER.

The *seven first* centuries were filled with a succession of triumphs.—GIBBON.

ARTICLES.

Definite article.

433. The **definite article** is repeated before each of two modifiers of the same noun, when the purpose is to call attention to the noun expressed and the one understood. In such a case two or more separate objects are usually indicated by the separation of the modifiers. Examples of this construction are,—

With a singular noun.

> The merit of *the Barb, the Spanish,* and *the English* breed is derived from a mixture of Arabian blood.—GIBBON.
>
> *The righteous* man is distinguished from *the unrighteous* by his desire and hope of justice.—RUSKIN.
>
> He seemed deficient in sympathy for concrete human things either on *the sunny* or *the stormy* side.—CARLYLE.
>
> It is difficult to imagine a greater contrast than that between *the first* and *the second* part of the volume.—*THE NATION*, No. 1508.

With a plural noun.

> There was also a fundamental difference of opinion as to whether the earliest cleavage was between *the Northern* and *the Southern* languages.—TAYLOR, *Origin of the Aryans.*

434. The same repetition of the article is sometimes found before nouns alone, to distinguish clearly, or to emphasize the meaning; as,—

> In every line of *the Philip* and *the Saul,* the greatest poems, I think, of the eighteenth century.—MACAULAY.

He is master of the two-fold Logos, *the thought* and *the word*, distinct, but inseparable from each other.—NEWMAN.

The flowers, and *the presents*, and *the trunks and bonnet boxes* ... having been arranged, the hour of parting came.—THACKERAY.

> The *not repeated. One object and several modifiers, with a singular noun.*

435. Frequently, however, the article is not repeated before each of two or more adjectives, as in Sec. 433, but is used with one only; as,—

Or fanciest thou *the red and yellow* Clothes-screen yonder is but of To-day, without a Yesterday or a To-morrow?—CARLYLE.

The lofty, melodious, and flexible language.—SCOTT.

The fairest and most loving wife in Greece.—TENNYSON.

> *Meaning same as in Sec. 433, with a plural noun.*

Neither can there be a much greater resemblance between *the ancient and modern* general views of the town.—HALLIWELL-PHILLIPPS.

At Talavera *the English and French* troops for a moment suspended their conflict.—MACAULAY.

The Crusades brought to the rising commonwealths of *the Adriatic and Tyrrhene* seas a large increase of wealth.—ID.

Here the youth of both sexes, of *the higher and middling* orders, were placed at a very tender age.—PRESCOTT.

> *Indefinite article.*

436. The **indefinite article** is used, like the definite article, to limit two or more modified nouns, only one of which is expressed. The article is repeated for the purpose of separating or emphasizing the modified nouns. Examples of this use are,—

We shall live *a better* and *a higher* and *a nobler* life.—BEECHER.

The difference between the products of *a well-disciplined* and those of *an uncultivated* understanding is often and admirably exhibited by our great dramatist.—S. T. Coleridge.

Let us suppose that the pillars succeed each other, *a round* and *a square* one alternately.—Burke.

As if the difference between *an accurate* and *an inaccurate* statement was not worth the trouble of looking into the most common book of reference.—Macaulay.

To every room there was *an open* and *a secret* passage.—Johnson.

Notice that in the above sentences (except the first) the noun expressed is in contrast with the modified noun omitted.

> *One article with several adjectives.*

437. Usually the article is not repeated when the several adjectives unite in describing one and the same noun. In the sentences of Secs. 433 and 436, one noun is expressed; yet the same word understood with the other adjectives has a different meaning (except in the first sentence of Sec. 436). But in the following sentences, as in the first three of Sec. 435, the adjectives assist each other in describing the same noun. It is easy to see the difference between the expressions "*a red-and-white* geranium," and "*a red and a white* geranium."

Examples of several adjectives describing the same object:—

To inspire us with *a free and quiet* mind.—B. Jonson.

Here and there *a desolate and uninhabited* house.—Dickens.

James was declared *a mortal and bloody* enemy.—Macaulay.

So wert thou born into a tuneful strain,
An early, rich, and inexhausted vein.
—Dryden.

> *For rhetorical effect.*

438. The indefinite article (compare Sec. 434) is used to lend special emphasis, interest, or clearness to each of several nouns; as,—

> James was declared *a* mortal and bloody *enemy, a tyrant, a murderer,* and *a usurper.*—MACAULAY.

> Thou hast spoken as *a patriot* and *a Christian.*—BULWER.

> He saw him in his mind's eye, *a collegian, a parliament man—a Baronet* perhaps.—THACKERAY.

VERBS.

CONCORD OF VERB AND SUBJECT IN NUMBER.

A broad and loose rule.

439. In English, the **number** of the verb follows the meaning rather than the form of its subject.

It will not do to state as a general rule that the verb agrees with its subject in person and number. This was spoken of in Part I., Sec. 276, and the following illustrations prove it.

The statements and illustrations of course refer to such verbs as have separate forms for singular and plural number.

Singular verb.

440. The **singular form** of the verb is used—

Subject of singular form.

(1) When the subject has a singular form and a singular meaning.

Such, then, *was* the earliest American *land.*—AGASSIZ.

He was certainly a happy fellow at this time.—G. ELIOT.

He sees that it is better to live in peace.—COOPER.

Collective noun of singular meaning.

(2) When the subject is a *collective noun* which represents a number of persons or things *taken as one unit*; as,—

The larger *breed* [of camels] *is* capable of transporting a weight of a thousand pounds.—GIBBON.

Another *school professes* entirely opposite principles.—*The Nation.*

In this work there *was* grouped around him *a score* of men.—W. Phillips

A *number* of jeweled paternosters *was* attached to her girdle.—Froude.

Something like a horse load of books *has* been written to prove that it was the beauty who blew up the booby.—Carlyle

This usage, like some others in this series, depends mostly on the writer's own judgment. Another writer might, for example, prefer a plural verb after *number* in Froude's sentence above.

> *Singulars connected by* or *or* nor.

(3) When the subject consists of two or more singular nouns connected by *or* or *nor*; as,—

It is by no means sure that either our *literature*, or the great intellectual *life* of our nation, *has* got already, without academies, all that academies can give.—M. Arnold.

Jesus is not dead, nor *John*, nor *Paul*, nor *Mahomet*. —Emerson.

> *Plural form and singular meaning.*

(4) When the subject is *plural in form*, but represents a number of things to be taken together as *forming one unit*; for example,—

Thirty-four years *affects* one's remembrance of some circumstances.—De Quincey.

Between ourselves, three pounds five shillings and two pence *is* no bad day's work.—Goldsmith.

Every twenty paces *gives* you the prospect of some villa; and every four hours, that of a large town.—Montague

Two thirds of this *is* mine by right.—SHERIDAN

The singular form is also used with book titles, other names, and other singulars of plural form; as,—

Politics *is* the only field now open for me.—WHITTIER.

"Sesame and Lilies" *is* Ruskin's creed for young girls.—CRITIC, No. 674

The Three Pigeons *expects* me down every moment.—GOLDSMITH.

> *Several singular subjects to one singular verb.*

(5) With *several singular subjects not* disjoined by *or* or *nor*, in the following cases:—

(*a*) Joined by *and*, but considered as meaning about the same thing, or as making up one general idea; as,—

In a word, all his conversation and knowledge *has been* in the female world—ADDISON.

The strength and glare of each [color] *is* considerably abated.—BURKE

To imagine that debating and logic *is* the triumph.—CARLYLE

In a world where even to fold and seal a letter adroitly *is* not the least of accomplishments.—DE QUINCEY

The genius and merit of a rising poet *was* celebrated.—GIBBON.

When the cause of ages and the fate of nations *hangs* upon the thread of a debate.—J. Q. ADAMS.

(*b*) Not joined by a conjunction, but each one emphatic, or considered as appositional; for example,—

The unbought grace of life, the cheap defense of nations, the nurse of manly sentiment and heroic enterprise, *is* gone.—

Burke.

A fever, a mutilation, a cruel disappointment, a loss of wealth, a loss of friends, *seems* at the moment unpaid loss.—Emerson

The author, the wit, the partisan, the fine gentleman, *does* not take the place of the man.—Id.

To receive presents or a bribe, to be guilty of collusion in any way with a suitor, *was* punished, in a judge, with death.—Prescott.

> *Subjects after the verb.*

This use of several subjects with a singular verb is especially frequent when the subjects are after the verb; as,—

There *is* a right and a wrong in them.—M Arnold.

There *is* a moving tone of voice, an impassioned countenance, an agitated gesture.—Burke

There *was* a steel headpiece, a cuirass, a gorget, and greaves, with a pair of gauntlets and a sword hanging beneath.—Hawthorne.

Then *comes* the "Why, sir!" and the "What then, sir?" and the "No, sir!"—Macaulay.

For wide *is* heard the thundering fray,
The rout, the ruin, the dismay.
—Scott.

(*c*) Joined by *as well as* (in this case the verb agrees with the first of the two, no matter if the second is plural); thus,—

Asia, as well as Europe, *was* dazzled.—Macaulay.

The oldest, as well as the newest, wine
Begins to stir itself.

—LONGFELLOW.

Her back, as well as sides, *was* like to crack.—BUTLER.

The Epic, as well as the Drama, *is* divided into tragedy and Comedy.—FIELDING

(*d*) When each of two or more singular subjects is preceded by *every, each, no, many a*, and such like adjectives.

Every fop, every boor, every valet, *is* a man of wit.—MACAULAY.

Every sound, every echo, *was* listened to for five hours.—DE QUINCEY

Every dome and hollow *has* the figure of Christ.—RUSKIN.

Each particular hue and tint *stands* by itself.—NEWMAN.

Every law and usage *was* a man's expedient.—EMERSON.

Here *is* no ruin, no discontinuity, no spent ball.—ID.

Every week, nay, almost every day, *was* set down in their calendar for some appropriate celebration.—PRESCOTT.

> *Plural verb.*

441. The **plural form** of the verb is used—

(1) When the subject is plural *in form and in meaning*; as,—

These *bits* of wood *were* covered on every square.—SWIFT.

Far, far away thy children *leave* the land.—GOLDSMITH.

The Arabian poets *were* the historians and moralists.—GIBBON.

(2) When the subject is a *collective noun* in which *the individuals* of the collection are thought of; as,—

A multitude *go* mad about it.—EMERSON.

A great number of people *were* collected at a vendue.—FRANKLIN.

All our household *are* at rest.—COLERIDGE.

A party of workmen *were* removing the horses.—LEW WALLACE

The fraternity *were* inclined to claim for him the honors of canonization.—SCOTT.

The travelers, of whom there *were* a number.—B. TAYLOR.

(3) When the subject consists of *several singulars connected by and*, making up a plural subject, for example,—

Only Vice and Misery *are* abroad.—CARLYLE

But its authorship, its date, and its history *are* alike a mystery to us.—FROUDE.

His clothes, shirt, and skin *were* all of the same color—SWIFT.

Aristotle and Longinus *are* better understood by him than Littleton or Coke.—ADDISON.

> *Conjunction omitted.*

The conjunction may be omitted, as in Sec. 440 (5, *b*), but the verb is plural, as with a subject of plural form.

A shady grove, a green pasture, a stream of fresh water, *are* sufficient to attract a colony.—GIBBON.

The Dauphin, the Duke of Berri, Philip of Anjou, *were* men of insignificant characters.—MACAULAY

(4) When a singular is joined with a plural by a disjunctive word, the verb agrees with the one nearest it; as,—

One or two of these perhaps *survive*.—THOREAU.

One or two persons in the crowd *were* insolent.—FROUDE.

One or two of the ladies *were* going to leave.—Addison

One or two of these old Cromwellian soldiers *were* still alive in the village.—Thackeray

One or two of whom *were* more entertaining.—De Quincey.

But notice the construction of this,—

A ray or two *wanders* into the darkness.—Ruskin.

AGREEMENT OF VERB AND SUBJECT IN PERSON.

General usage.

442. If there is only one person in the subject, the ending of the verb indicates the person of its subject; that is, in those few cases where there are forms for different persons: as,—

Never once *didst* thou revel in the vision.—De Quincey.

Romanism wisely *provides* for the childish in men.—Lowell.

It *hath* been said my Lord would never take the oath.—Thackeray.

Second or third and first person in the subject.

443. If the subject is made up of the first person joined with the second or third by *and*, the verb takes the construction of the first person, the subject being really equivalent to *we*; as,—

I flatter myself you and I *shall* meet again.—Smollett.

You and I *are* farmers; we never talk politics.—D. Webster.

Ah, brother! only I and thou
Are left of all that circle now.
—Whittier.

You and I *are* tolerably modest people.—THACKERAY.

Cocke and I *have* felt it in our bones—GAMMER GURTON'S NEEDLE

> *With adversative or disjunctive connectives.*

444. When the subjects, of different persons, are connected by adversative or disjunctive conjunctions, the verb usually agrees with the pronoun nearest to it; for example,—

Neither you nor I *should* be a bit the better or wiser.—RUSKIN.

If she or you *are* resolved to be miserable.—GOLDSMITH.

Nothing which Mr. Pattison or I *have* said.—M. ARNOLD.

Not Altamont, but thou, *hadst* been my lord.—ROWE.

Not I, but thou, his blood *dost* shed.—BYRON.

This construction is at the best a little awkward. It is avoided either by using a verb which has no forms for person (as, "He or I *can* go," "She or you *may* be sure," etc.), or by rearranging the sentence so as to throw each subject before its proper person form (as, "You *would* not be wiser, nor *should* I;" or, "I *have* never said so, nor *has* she").

> *Exceptional examples.*

445. The following illustrate exceptional usage, which it is proper to mention; but the student is cautioned to follow the regular usage rather than the unusual and irregular.

Exercise.

Change each of the following sentences to accord with standard usage, as illustrated above (Secs. **440-444**):—

1.

And sharp Adversity will teach at last

> Man,—and, as we would hope,—perhaps the devil,
> That neither of their intellects are vast.
> —BYRON.

2. Neither of them, in my opinion, give so accurate an idea of the man as a statuette in bronze.—TROLLOPE.

3. How each of these professions are crowded.—ADDISON.

4. Neither of their counselors were to be present.—ID.

5. Either of them are equally good to the person to whom they are significant.—EMERSON.

6. Neither the red nor the white are strong and glaring.—BURKE.

7. A lampoon or a satire do not carry in them robbery or murder.—ADDISON.

8. Neither of the sisters were very much deceived.—THACKERAY.

9.

> Nor wood, nor tree, nor bush are there,
> Her course to intercept.
> —SCOTT.

10. Both death and I am found eternal.—MILTON.

11. In ascending the Mississippi the party was often obliged to wade through morasses; at last they came upon the district of Little Prairie. —G. BANCROFT.

12. In a word, the whole nation seems to be running out of their wits. —SMOLLETT.

SEQUENCE OF TENSES (VERBS AND VERBALS).

Lack of logical sequence in verbs.

446. If one or more verbs depend on some leading verb, each should be in the tense that will convey the meaning intended by the writer.

In this sentence from Defoe, "I expected every wave would have swallowed us up," the verb *expected* looks forward to something in the future, while *would have swallowed* represents something completed in past time: hence the meaning intended was, "I expected every wave *would swallow*" etc.

> *Also in verbals.*

In the following sentence, the infinitive also fails to express the exact thought:—

> I had hoped never to have seen the statues again.—MACAULAY.

The trouble is the same as in the previous sentence; *to have seen* should be changed to *to see*, for exact connection. Of course, if the purpose were to represent a prior fact or completed action, the perfect infinitive would be the very thing.

It should be remarked, however, that such sentences as those just quoted are in keeping with the older idea of the unity of the sentence. The present rule is recent.

Exercise.

Explain whether the verbs and infinitives in the following sentences convey the right meaning; if not, change them to a better form:—

> 1. I gave one quarter to Ann, meaning, on my return, to have divided with her whatever might remain.—DE QUINCEY

> 2. I can't sketch "The Five Drapers," ... but can look and be thankful to have seen such a masterpiece.—THACKERAY.

> 3. He would have done more wisely to have left them to find their own apology than to have given reasons which seemed paradoxes.—R. W. CHURCH.

> 4. The propositions of William are stated to have contained a proposition for a compromise.—PALGRAVE

5. But I found I wanted a stock of words, which I thought I should have acquired before that time.—FRANKLIN

6. I could even have suffered them to have broken Everet Ducking's head.—IRVING.

INDIRECT DISCOURSE.

> *Definitions.*

447. Direct discourse—that is, a direct quotation or a direct question—means the identical words the writer or speaker used; as,—

"I hope you have not killed him?" said Amyas.—KINGSLEY.

Indirect discourse means reported speech,—the thoughts of a writer or speaker put in the words of the one reporting them.

> *Two samples of indirect discourse.*

448. Indirect discourse may be of two kinds:—

(1) Following the thoughts and also the exact words as far as consistent with the rules of logical sequence of verbs.

(2) Merely a concise representation of the original words, not attempting to follow the entire quotation.

The following examples of both are from De Quincey:—

> *Indirect.*

1. Reyes remarked that it was not in his power to oblige the clerk as to that, but that he could oblige him by cutting his throat.

> *Direct.*

His exact words were, "I *cannot* oblige *you* ..., but I *can* oblige *you* by cutting *your* throat."

Indirect.

Her prudence whispered eternally, that safety there was none for her until she had laid the Atlantic between herself and St. Sebastian's.

Direct.

She thought to herself, "Safety there *is* none for *me* until *I* have laid," etc.

Summary of the expressions.

2. Then he laid bare the unparalleled ingratitude of such a step. Oh, the unseen treasure that had been spent upon that girl! Oh, the untold sums of money that he had sunk in that unhappy speculation!

Direct synopsis.

The substance of his lamentation was, "Oh, unseen treasure *has* been spent upon that girl! Untold sums of money *have I* sunk," etc.

449. From these illustrations will be readily seen the grammatical changes made in transferring from direct to indirect discourse. Remember the following facts:—

(1) Usually the main, introductory verb is in the past tense.

(2) The indirect quotation is usually introduced by *that*, and the indirect question by *whether* or *if*, or regular interrogatives.

(3) Verbs in the present-tense form are changed to the past-tense form. This includes the auxiliaries *be, have, will,* etc. The past tense is sometimes changed to the past perfect.

(4) The pronouns of the first and second persons are all changed to the third person. Sometimes it is clearer to introduce the antecedent of the pronoun instead.

Other examples of indirect discourse have been given in Part I., under interrogative pronouns, interrogative adverbs, and the subjunctive mood of verbs.

Exercise.

Rewrite the following extract from Irving's "Sketch Book," and change it to a direct quotation:—

> He assured the company that it was a fact, handed down from his ancestor the historian, that the Catskill Mountains had always been haunted by strange beings; that it was affirmed that the great Hendrick Hudson, the first discoverer of the river and country, kept a kind of vigil there every twenty years, with his crew of the Half-moon, being permitted in this way to revisit the scenes of his enterprise, and keep a guardian eye upon the river and the great city called by his name; that his father had once seen them in their old Dutch dresses playing at ninepins in a hollow of the mountain; and that he himself had heard, one summer afternoon, the sound of their balls, like distant peals of thunder.

VERBALS.

PARTICIPLES.

> *Careless use of the participial phrase.*

450. The following sentences illustrate a misuse of the participial phrase:—

> Pleased with the "Pilgrim's Progress," my first collection was of John Bunyan's works.—B. FRANKLIN.

> My farm consisted of about twenty acres of excellent land, having given a hundred pounds for my predecessor's goodwill.—GOLDSMITH.

> Upon asking how he had been taught the art of a cognoscente so suddenly, he assured me that nothing was more easy.—ID.

> Having thus run through the causes of the sublime, my first observation will be found nearly true.—BURKE

> He therefore remained silent till he had repeated a paternoster, being the course which his confessor had enjoined.—SCOTT

Compare with these the following:—

> *A correct example.*

> Going yesterday to dine with an old acquaintance, I had the misfortune to find his whole family very much dejected.—ADDISON.

> *Notice this.*

The trouble is, in the sentences first quoted, that the main subject of the sentence is not the same word that would be the subject of the participle, if this were expanded into a verb.

> *Correction.*

Consequently one of two courses must be taken,—either change the participle to a verb with its appropriate subject, leaving the principal statement as it is; or change the principal proposition so it shall make logical connection with the participial phrase.

For example, the first sentence would be, either "*As I was* pleased, ... my first collection was," etc., or "Pleased with the 'Pilgrim's Progress,' I made my first collection John Bunyan's works."

Exercise.—Rewrite the other four sentences so as to correct the careless use of the participial phrase.

INFINITIVES.

> *Adverb between* to *and the infinitive.*

451. There is a construction which is becoming more and more common among good writers,—the placing an adverb between *to* of the infinitive and the infinitive itself. The practice is condemned by many grammarians, while defended or excused by others. Standard writers often use it, and often, purposely or not, avoid it.

The following two examples show the adverb before the infinitive:—

> *The more common usage.*

>> He handled it with such nicety of address as sufficiently *to show* that he fully understood the business.—SCOTT.

>> It is a solemn, universal assertion, deeply *to be kept* in mind by all sects.—RUSKIN.

This is the more common arrangement; yet frequently the desire seems to be to get the adverb snugly against the infinitive, to modify it as closely and clearly as possible.

Exercise.

In the following citations, see if the adverbs can be placed before or after the infinitive and still modify it as clearly as they now do:—

> 1. There are, then, many things *to be* carefully *considered*, if a strike is to succeed.—LAUGHLIN.

> 2. That the mind may not have to go backwards and forwards in order *to* rightly *connect* them.—HERBERT SPENCER.

3. It may be easier to bear along all the qualifications of an idea ... than *to* first imperfectly *conceive* such idea.—ID.

4. In works of art, this kind of grandeur, which consists in multitude, is *to be* very cautiously *admitted*.—BURKE.

5. That virtue which requires *to be* ever *guarded* is scarcely worth the sentinel.—GOLDSMITH.

6. Burke said that such "little arts and devices" were not *to be* wholly *condemned*.—*The Nation*, No. 1533.

7. I wish the reader *to* clearly *understand*.—RUSKIN.

8. Transactions which seem *to be* most widely *separated* from one another.—DR. BLAIR.

9. Would earnestly advise them for their good to order this paper *to be* punctually *served up*.—ADDISON.

10. A little sketch of his, in which a cannon ball is supposed *to have* just *carried off* the head of an aide-de-camp.—TROLLOPE.

11. The ladies seem *to have been* expressly *created* to form helps meet for such gentlemen.—MACAULAY.

12. Sufficient to disgust a people whose manners were beginning *to be* strongly *tinctured* with austerity.—ID.

13. The spirits, therefore, of those opposed to them seemed *to be* considerably *damped* by their continued success.—SCOTT.

ADVERBS.

> *Position of* only, even, *etc.*

452. A very careful writer will so place the modifiers of a verb that the reader will not mistake the meaning.

The rigid rule in such a case would be, to put the modifier in such a position that the reader not only can understand the meaning intended, but *cannot misunderstand* the thought. Now, when such adverbs as *only, even,* etc., are used, they are usually placed in a strictly correct position, if they modify single words; but they are often removed from the exact position, if they modify phrases or clauses: for example, from Irving, "The site is *only* to be traced by fragments of bricks, china, and earthenware." Here *only* modifies the phrase *by fragments of bricks*, etc., but it is placed before the infinitive. This misplacement of the adverb can be detected only by analysis of the sentence.

Exercise.

Tell what the adverb modifies in each quotation, and see if it is placed in the proper position:—

1. Only the name of one obscure epigrammatist has been embalmed for us in the verses of his rival.—PALGRAVE.

2. Do you remember pea shooters? I think we only had them on going home for holidays.—THACKERAY.

3. Irving could only live very modestly. He could only afford to keep one old horse.—ID.

4. The arrangement of this machinery could only be accounted for by supposing the motive power to have been steam.—WENDELL PHILLIPS.

5. Such disputes can only be settled by arms.—*Id.*

6. I have only noted one or two topics which I thought most likely to interest an American reader.—N. P. Willis.

7. The silence of the first night at the farmhouse,—stillness broken only by two whippoorwills.—Higginson.

8. My master, to avoid a crowd, would suffer only thirty people at a time to see me.—Swift.

9. In relating these and the following laws, I would only be understood to mean the original institutions.—*Id.*

10. The perfect loveliness of a woman's countenance can only consist in that majestic peace which is founded in the memory of happy and useful years.—Ruskin.

11. In one of those celestial days it seems a poverty that we can only spend it once.—Emerson.

12. My lord was only anxious as long as his wife's anxious face or behavior seemed to upbraid him.—Thackeray.

13. He shouted in those clear, piercing tones that could be even heard among the roaring of the cannon.—Cooper.

14. His suspicions were not even excited by the ominous face of Gérard.—Motley.

15. During the whole course of his administration, he scarcely befriended a single man of genius.—Macaulay.

16. I never remember to have felt an event more deeply than his death.—Sydney Smith.

17. His last journey to Cannes, whence he was never destined to return.—Mrs. Grote.

USE OF DOUBLE NEGATIVES.

> *The old usage.*

453. In Old and Middle English, two negatives strengthened a negative idea; for example,—

> He *nevere* yet *no* vileineye *ne* sayde,
> In al his lyf unto *no* maner wight.
> —Chaucer.

> *No* sonne, were he never so old of yeares, might *not* marry. —
> Ascham.

The first of these is equivalent to "He didn't never say no villainy in all his life to no manner of man,"—four negatives.

This idiom was common in the older stages of the language, and is still kept in vulgar English; as,—

> I tell you she *ain'* been *nowhar* ef she don' know we all. —Page, in *Ole Virginia*.

> There *weren't no* pies to equal hers.—Mrs. Stowe.

> *Exceptional use.*

There are sometimes found two negatives in modern English with a negative effect, when one of the negatives is a connective. This, however, is not common.

> I never did see him again, *nor never* shall.—De Quincey.

> However, I did *not* act so hastily, *neither*.—Defoe.

> The prosperity of no empire, *nor* the grandeur of *no* king, can so agreeably affect, etc.—Burke.

> *Regular law of negative in modern English.*

But, under the influence of Latin syntax, the usual way of regarding the question now is, that *two negatives are equivalent to an affirmative,* denying each other.

Therefore, if two negatives are found together, it is a sign of ignorance or carelessness, or else a purpose to make an affirmative effect. In the latter case, one of the negatives is often a prefix; as *in*frequent, *un*common.

Exercise.

Tell whether the two or more negatives are properly used in each of the following sentences, and why:—

1. The red men were not so infrequent visitors of the English settlements.—Hawthorne.

2. "Huldy was so up to everything about the house, that the doctor didn't miss nothin' in a temporal way."—Mrs. Stowe.

3. Her younger sister was a wide-awake girl, who hadn't been to school for nothing.—Holmes.

4. You will find no battle which does not exhibit the most cautious circumspection.—Bayne.

5. Not only could man not acquire such information, but ought not to labor after it.—Grote.

6. There is no thoughtful man in America who would not consider a war with England the greatest of calamities.—Lowell.

7. In the execution of this task, there is no man who would not find it an arduous effort.—Hamilton.

8. "A weapon," said the King, "well worthy to confer honor, nor has it been laid on an undeserving shoulder."—Scott.

CONJUNCTIONS.

> And who, and which.

454. The sentences given in Secs. 419 and 420 on the connecting of pronouns with different expressions may again be referred to here, as the use of the conjunction, as well as of the pronoun, should be scrutinized.

> *Choice and proper position of correlatives.*

455. The most frequent mistakes in using conjunctions are in handling correlatives, especially *both ... and, neither ... nor, either ... or, not only ... but, not merely ... but (also)*.

The following examples illustrate the correct use of correlatives as to both choice of words and position:—

> *Whether* at war *or* at peace, there we were, a standing menace to all earthly paradises of that kind.—LOWELL.
>
> These idols of wood can *neither* hear *nor* feel.—PRESCOTT.
>
> *Both* the common soldiery *and* their leaders and commanders lowered on each other as if their union had not been more essential than ever, *not only* to the success of their common cause, *but* to their own safety.—SCOTT.

> *Things to be watched.*

In these examples it will be noticed that *nor*, not *or* is the proper correlative of *neither*; and that all correlatives in a sentence ought to have corresponding positions: that is, if the last precedes a verb, the first ought to be placed before a verb; if the second precedes a phrase, the first should also. This is necessary to make the sentence clear and symmetrical.

> *Correction.*

In the sentence, "I am *neither* in spirits to enjoy it, *or* to reply to it," both of the above requirements are violated. The word *neither* in such a case had better be changed to *not ... either,*—"I am not in spirits *either* to enjoy it, *or* to reply to it."

Besides *neither ... or*, even *neither ... nor* is often changed to *not—either ... or* with advantage, as the negation is sometimes too far from the verb to which it belongs.

A noun may be preceded by one of the correlatives, and an equivalent pronoun by the other. The sentence, "This loose and inaccurate manner of speaking has misled us *both* in the theory of taste *and* of morals," may be changed to "This loose ... misled us *both* in the theory of taste *and* in *that* of morals."

Exercise.

Correct the following sentences:—

1. An ordinary man would neither have incurred the danger of succoring Essex, nor the disgrace of assailing him.—MACAULAY.

2. Those ogres will stab about and kill not only strangers, but they will outrage, murder, and chop up their own kin.—THACKERAY.

3. In the course of his reading (which was neither pursued with that seriousness or that devout mind which such a study requires) the youth found himself, etc.—ID.

4. I could neither bear walking nor riding in a carriage over its pebbled streets.—FRANKLIN.

5. Some exceptions, that can neither be dissembled nor eluded, render this mode of reasoning as indiscreet as it is superfluous.—GIBBON.

6. They will, too, not merely interest children, but grown-up persons.—*WESTMINSTER REVIEW.*

7. I had even the satisfaction to see her lavish some kind looks upon my unfortunate son, which the other could neither extort by his fortune nor assiduity.—GOLDSMITH.

8. This was done probably to show that he was neither ashamed of his name or family.—ADDISON.

> Try and *for* try to.

456. Occasionally there is found the expression *try and* instead of the better authorized *try to*; as,—

We will try *and* avoid personalities altogether.—THACKERAY.

Did any of you ever try *and* read "Blackmore's Poems"?—ID.

Try *and* avoid the pronoun.—BAIN.

We will try *and* get a clearer notion of them.—RUSKIN.

> But what.

457. Instead of the subordinate conjunction *that, but,* or *but that,* or the negative relative *but,* we sometimes find the bulky and needless *but what.* Now, it is possible to use *but what* when *what* is a relative pronoun, as, "He never had any money *but what* he absolutely needed;" but in the following sentences *what* usurps the place of a conjunction.

Exercise.

In the following sentences, substitute *that, but,* or *but that* for the words *but what*:—

1. The doctor used to say 'twas her young heart, and I don't know *but what* he was right.—S. O. JEWETT.

2. At the first stroke of the pickax it is ten to one *but what* you are taken up for a trespass.—BULWER.

3. There are few persons of distinction *but what* can hold conversation in both languages.—SWIFT.

4. Who knows *but what* there might be English among those sun-browned half-naked masses of panting wretches?—KINGSLEY.

5. No little wound of the kind ever came to him *but what* he disclosed it at once.—TROLLOPE.

6. They are not so distant from the camp of Saladin *but what* they might be in a moment surprised.—SCOTT.

PREPOSITIONS.

458. As to the placing of a preposition after its object in certain cases, see Sec. 305.

> Between *and* among.

459. In the primary meaning of **between** and **among** there is a sharp distinction, as already seen in Sec. 313; but in Modern English the difference is not so marked.

Between is used most often with two things only, but still it is frequently used in speaking of several objects, some relation or connection between two at a time being implied.

Among is used in the same way as *amid* (though not with exactly the same meaning), several objects being spoken of in the aggregate, no separation or division by twos being implied.

Examples of the distinctive use of the two words:—

> *Two things.*

>> The contentions that arise *between* the parson and the squire.—ADDISON.

>> We reckoned the improvements of the art of war *among* the triumphs of science.—EMERSON.

Examples of the looser use of *between*:—

> *A number of things.*

>> Natural objects affect us by the laws of that connection which Providence has established *between* certain motions of bodies.—BURKE.

> Hence the differences *between* men in natural endowment are insignificant in comparison with their common wealth.—EMERSON.
>
> They maintain a good correspondence *between* those wealthy societies of men that are divided from one another by seas and oceans.—ADDISON.
>
> Looking up at its deep-pointed porches and the dark places *between* their pillars where there were statues once.—RUSKIN
>
> What have I, a soldier of the Cross, to do with recollections of war *betwixt* Christian nations?—SCOTT.

Two groups or one and a group.

Also *between* may express relation or connection in speaking of two groups of objects, or one object and a group; as,—

> A council of war is going on beside the watch fire, *between* the three adventurers and the faithful Yeo.—KINGSLEY.
>
> The great distinction *between* teachers sacred or literary,—*between* poets like Herbert and poets like Pope,—*between* philosophers like Spinoza, Kant, and Coleridge, and philosophers like Locke, Paley, Mackintosh, and Stewart, etc.—EMERSON.

460. Certain words are followed by particular prepositions.

Some of these words show by their composition what preposition should follow. Such are *absolve, involve, different.*

Some of them have, by custom, come to take prepositions not in keeping with the original meaning of the words. Such are *derogatory, averse.*

Many words take one preposition to express one meaning, and another to convey a different meaning; as, *correspond, confer.*

And yet others may take several prepositions indifferently to express the same meaning.

> List I.: Words with particular prepositions.

461.

LIST I.

Absolve *from*.
Abhorrent *to*.
Accord *with*.
Acquit *of*.
Affinity *between*.
Averse *to*.
Bestow *on* (*upon*).
Conform *to*.
Comply *with*.
Conversant *with*.
Dependent *on* (*upon*).
Different *from*.
Dissent *from*.
Derogatory *to*.
Deprive *of*.
Independent *of*.
Involve *in*.

"Different *to*" is frequently heard in spoken English in England, and sometimes creeps into standard books, but it is not good usage.

> List II.: Words taking different prepositions for different meanings.

462.

LIST II.

Agree *with* (a person).
Agree *to* (a proposal).
Change *for* (a thing).
Change *with* (a person).

Change *to* (become).
Confer *with* (talk with).
Confer *on* (*upon*) (give to).
Confide *in* (trust in).
Confide *to* (intrust to).
Correspond *with* (write to).
Correspond *to* (a thing).
Differ *from* (note below).
Differ *with* (note below).
Disappointed *in* (a thing obtained).
Disappointed *of* (a thing not obtained).
Reconcile *to* (note below).
Reconcile *with* (note below).
A taste *of* (food).
A taste *for* (art, etc.).

"Correspond *with*" is sometimes used of things, as meaning *to be in keeping with*.

"Differ *from*" is used in speaking of unlikeness between things or persons; "differ *from*" and "differ *with*" are both used in speaking of persons disagreeing as to opinions.

"Reconcile *to*" is used with the meaning of *resigned to,* as, "The exile became reconciled *to* his fate;" also of persons, in the sense of making friends with, as, "The king is reconciled *to* his minister." "Reconcile *with*" is used with the meaning of *make to agree with,* as, "The statement must be reconciled *with* his previous conduct."

> *List III.: Words taking anyone of several prepositions for the same meaning.*

463.

LIST III.

Die *by*, die *for*, die *from*, die *of*, die *with*.
Expect *of*, expect *from*.
Part *from*, part *with*.

Illustrations of "die *of*," "die *from*," etc.:—

> "*Die* of."

The author died *of* a fit of apoplexy.—Boswell.

People do not die *of* trifling little colds.—Austen

Fifteen officers died *of* fever in a day.—Macaulay.

It would take me long to die *of* hunger.—G. Eliot.

She died *of* hard work, privation, and ill treatment.—Burnett.

> "*Die* from."

She saw her husband at last literally die *from* hunger.—Bulwer.

He died at last without disease, simply *from* old age. —Athenæum.

No one *died from* want at Longfeld.—Chambers' Journal.

> "*Die* with."

She would have been ready to die *with* shame.—G. Eliot.

I am positively dying *with* hunger.—Scott.

I thought the two Miss Flamboroughs would have died *with* laughing.—Goldsmith.

I wish that the happiest here may not die *with* envy.—Pope.

> "*Die* for." (*in behalf of*).

Take thought and die *for* Cæsar.—Shakespeare.

One of them said he would die *for* her.—Goldsmith.

It is a man of quality who dies *for* her.—Addison.

> "*Die* for." (*because of*).

Who, as Cervantes informs us, died *for* love of the fair Marcella.—Fielding.

Some officers had died *for* want of a morsel of bread.—Macaulay.

> "*Die* by." (*material cause, instrument*).

If I meet with any of 'em, they shall die *by* this hand.—Thackeray.

He must purge himself to the satisfaction of a vigilant tribunal or die *by* fire.—Macaulay.

He died *by* suicide before he completed his eighteenth year.—Shaw.

464. Illustrations of "expect *of*," "expect *from:*"—

> "*Expect* of."

What do I expect *of* Dublin?—Punch.

That is more than I expected *of* you.—Scott.

Of Doctor P. nothing better was to be expected.—Poe.

Not knowing what might be expected *of* men in general.—G. Eliot.

> "*Expect* from."

She will expect more attention *from* you, as my friend.—Walpole.

There was a certain grace and decorum hardly to be expected *from* a man.—Macaulay.

I have long expected something remarkable *from* you.—G. Eliot.

465. "Part *with*" is used with both persons and things, but "part *from*" is less often found in speaking of things.

Illustrations of "part *with*," "part *from*:"—

> *"Part* with."

He was fond of everybody that he was used to, and hated to part *with* them.—Austen.

Cleveland was sorry to part *with* him.—Bulwer.

I can part *with* my children for their good.—Dickens.

I part *with* all that grew so near my heart.—Waller.

> *"Part* from."

To part *from* you would be misery.—Marryat.

I have just seen her, just parted *from* her.—Bulwer.

Burke parted *from* him with deep emotion.—Macaulay.

His precious bag, which he would by no means part *from*.—G. Eliot.

> *Kind* in *you, kind* of *you.*

466. With words implying behavior or disposition, either *of* or *in* is used indifferently, as shown in the following quotations:—

> Of.

It was a little bad *of* you.—Trollope.

How cruel *of* me!—Collins.

He did not think it handsome *of* you.—BULWER.

But this is idle *of* you.—TENNYSON.

> *In.*

Very natural *in* Mr. Hampden.—CARLYLE.

It will be anything but shrewd *in* you.—DICKENS.

That is very unreasonable *in* a person so young.—BEACONSFIELD.

I am wasting your whole morning—too bad *in* me.—BULWER.

Miscellaneous Examples for Correction.

1. Can you imagine Indians or a semi-civilized people engaged on a work like the canal connecting the Mediterranean and the Red seas?

2. In the friction between an employer and workman, it is commonly said that his profits are high.

3. None of them are in any wise willing to give his life for the life of his chief.

4. That which can be done with perfect convenience and without loss, is not always the thing that most needs to be done, or which we are most imperatively required to do.

5. Art is neither to be achieved by effort of thinking, nor explained by accuracy of speaking.

6. To such as thee the fathers owe their fame.

7. We tread upon the ancient granite that first divided the waters into a northern and southern ocean.

8. Thou tread'st, with seraphims, the vast abyss.

9. Eustace had slipped off his long cloak, thrown it over Amyas's head, and ran up the alley.

10. This narrative, tedious perhaps, but which the story renders necessary, may serve to explain the state of intelligence betwixt the lovers.

11. To the shame and eternal infamy of whomsoever shall turn back from the plow on which he hath laid his hand!

12. The noise of vast cataracts, raging storms, thunder, or artillery, awake a great and awful sensation in the mind.

13. The materials and ornaments ought neither to be white, nor green, nor yellow, nor blue, nor of a pale red.

14. This does not prove that an idea of use and beauty are the same thing, or that they are any way dependent on each other.

15.

> And were I anything but what I am,
> I would wish me only he.

16. But every man may know, and most of us do know, what is a just and unjust act.

17. You have seen Cassio and she together.

18. We shall shortly see which is the fittest object of scorn, you or me.

19. Richard glared round him with an eye that seemed to seek an enemy, and from which the angry nobles shrunk appalled.

20. It comes to whomsoever will put off what is foreign and proud.

21. The difference between the just and unjust procedure does not lie in the number of men hired, but in the price paid to them.

22. The effect of proportion and fitness, so far at least as they proceed from a mere consideration of the work itself, produce approbation, the acquiescence of the understanding.

23. When the glass or liquor are transparent, the light is sometimes softened in the passage.

24. For there nor yew nor cypress spread their gloom.

25. Every one of these letters are in my name.

26. Neither of them are remarkable for precision.

27. Squares, triangles, and other angular figures, are neither beautiful to the sight nor feeling.

28. There is not one in a thousand of these human souls that cares to think where this estate is, or how beautiful it is, or what kind of life they are to lead in it.

29. Dryden and Rowe's manner are quite out of fashion.

30. We were only permitted to stop for refreshment once.

31. The sight of the manner in which the meals were served were enough to turn our stomach.

32. The moody and savage state of mind of the sullen and ambitious man are admirably drawn.

33. Surely none of our readers are so unfortunate as not to know some man or woman who carry this atmosphere of peace and good-will about with them. (Sec. 411.)

34. Friday, whom he thinks would be better than a dog, and almost as good as a pony.

35. That night every man of the boat's crew, save Amyas, were down with raging fever.

36. These kind of books fill up the long tapestry of history with little bits of detail which give human interest to it.

37. I never remember the heather so rich and abundant.

38. These are scattered along the coast for several hundred miles, in conditions of life that seem forbidding enough, but which are accepted without complaint by the inhabitants themselves.

39. Between each was an interval where lay a musket.

40. He had four children, and it was confidently expected that they would receive a fortune of at least $200,000 between them.

FOOTNOTES:

[1] More for convenience than for absolute accuracy, the stages of our language have been roughly divided into three:—

(1) Old English (with Anglo-Saxon) down to the twelfth century.

(2) Middle English, from about the twelfth century to the sixteenth century.

(3) Modern English, from about 1500 to the present time.